JESUS' BIRTH

Study by Michael Usey
Commentary by Cecil Sherman

Free downloadable Teaching Guide for this study available at

NextSunday.com/teachingguides

NextSunday Resources
6316 Peake Road
Macon, Georgia 31210-3960
1-800-747-3016
©2018 by NextSunday Resources
All rights reserved.

TABLE OF CONTENTS

Jesus' Birth

HOW TO USE THIS STUDY

NextSunday Resources Adult Bible Studies are designed to help adults study Scripture seriously within the context of the larger Christian tradition and, through that process, find their faith renewed, challenged, and strengthened. We study the Scriptures because we believe they affect our current lives in important ways. Each study contains the following three components:

Study Guide

Each study guide lesson is arranged in four movements:

Remembering provides a frame of reference for the Scriptures.

Studying is centered on giving the biblical material in-depth attention while often surrounding it with helpful insights from theology, ethics, church history, and other areas.

Understanding helps us find relevant connections between our lives and the biblical message.

What About Me? provides brief statements that help unite life issues with the meaning of the biblical text.

Commentary

Each study guide lesson is accompanied by an additional, in-depth commentary on the biblical material. Written by a different author than the study guide, each commentary gives the opportunity for learners to approach the Scripture text from a separate but complementary viewpoint.

Teaching Guide

In addition to the provided study guide and commentary, *NextSunday Resources* also provides a *free* downloadable teaching guide, available at NextSunday.com. Each teaching guide gives the teacher tools for focusing on the content of each study guide lesson through additional commentary and Bible background information. Through teacher helps and teaching options, each teaching guide also provides substance for variety and choice in the preparation of each lesson.

NextSunday
Resources

STUDY INTRODUCTION

Many Christian churches use the Revised Common Lectionary [RCL] to determine which Scriptures to read in worship on Sunday mornings. The Lectionary system has informed Christian worship since the early days after the time of Jesus, not only calling believers to passages they might otherwise overlook, but also serving as a means of retelling the miraculous story of God's work. As you probably already know, the Christian year begins with the Advent season. The RCL offers a set of four readings (Old Testament, Psalms, Epistle, and Gospel) for each Sunday of the year, based on a three-year cycle with the titles of Years A, B, and C. The Gospel readings from Year A are derived largely from Matthew, Year B's from Mark and John, and Year C's from Luke.

This Advent study will follow Year C, and the majority of readings will originate from Luke's story of Jesus. Generally, the RCL readings for Advent follow this four-week pattern: Week 1, apocalyptic texts, or those that speak of Christ's return; Week 2, John the Baptizer's introduction; Week 3, the announcement to Mary of Jesus' pending birth; and Week 4, a description of John's impact or preaching.

Keep in mind, however, that this progression ignores the fact that one of our Gospels, namely Luke's, contains a full account of the events leading up to Jesus' birth. He starts from the very beginning, nine months before John's conception, and in fact, tells his account in full detail. Luke's narrative remembers the story of the angelic messenger who announced the coming of God into our world.

Too often we are a people who profess that God lives, yet somehow we still manage to forget that God acts among us. Mary knew that truth all too well. Her willing acceptance of the divine plan served as a means for God to walk among God's people. God's presence in Mary's life birthed an incredible joy that was shared by her cousin Elizabeth. We, too, may share in this joy, especially during Advent as we remember that God comes to *us* as well. As Luke recounts that the shepherds joyfully told the story of Jesus' birth, he also reminds us that *all* believers—whether ancient or contemporary—are invited to testify to the joy of Christ. So this study, as we wait for the birth of the Messiah, Luke helps us remember.

HUSHED BY AN ANGEL

Luke 1:5-25

Central Question

Which of God's gifts do you have difficulty accepting?

Scripture

Luke 1:11-25 Then there appeared to him an angel of the Lord, standing at the right side of the altar of incense. 12 When Zechariah saw him, he was terrified; and fear overwhelmed him. 13 But the angel said to him, "Do not be afraid, Zechariah, for your prayer has been heard. Your wife Elizabeth will bear you a son, and you will name him John. 14 You will have joy and glad-ness, and many will rejoice at his birth, 15 for he will be great in the sight of the Lord. He must never drink wine or strong drink; even before his birth he will be filled with the Holy Spirit. 16 He will turn many of the people of Israel to the Lord their God. 17 With the spirit and power of Elijah he will go before him, to turn the hearts of parents to their children, and the disobedient to the wisdom of the righteous, to make ready a people prepared for the Lord." 18 Zechariah said to the angel, "How will I know that this is so? For I am an old man, and my wife is getting on in years." 19 The angel replied, "I am Gabriel. I stand in the pres-ence of God, and I have been sent to speak to you and to bring you this good news. 20 But now, because you did not believe my words, which will be fulfilled in their time, you will become mute, unable to speak, until the day these things occur." 21 Meanwhile the people were waiting for Zechariah, and wondered at his delay in the sanctuary. 22 When he did come out, he could not speak to them, and they realized that he had seen a vision in the sanctuary. He kept motioning to them and remained unable to speak. 23 When his time of service was ended, he went to his home. 24 After those days his wife Elizabeth conceived, and for five months she remained in seclusion. She said, 25 "This is what the Lord has done for me when he looked favorably on me and took away the disgrace I have endured among my people."

Remembering

Luke's account of Jesus' life starts at the very beginning. The first four verses of chapter 1 compose a single, wonderfully written Greek sentence in which the author thanks Theophilus. Scholars have speculated that Theophilus might have been a real person, perhaps Luke's patron, or maybe even a relatively new Christian who just needed to hear the story of Christ from a Jewish-Christian perspective. Then again, since the name "Theophilus" means literally "God-lover," it is also just as possible that Luke is addressing his Gospel to anyone who loves God.

You will also note that the author never actually identifies himself as "Luke." In fact, the titles which have come to be commonly accepted in regards to the Gospels (called "superscriptions") were not even used on the original versions. Even so, there is no good reason not to use the traditional title: Luke's Gospel.

As evidenced by his introduction, Luke is well aware of some of the other stories about Jesus: *Since many have undertaken to set down an orderly account...* (1:1). In fact, Luke starts off by discussing his sources, a variety of stories that according to him were "handed down" from "eyewitnesses" (1:2). However, as you will notice, never does he claim to be an eyewitness himself.

We cannot say for sure to whom Luke's Gospel was written, but likely it was addressed to Jewish-Christians—known as "Diaspora" Jews—living outside of Palestine at the time. Not only is Luke's writing style excellent, but his command of the Greek language is just as superb. He recounts episodes from Jesus' life in the language and manner of the Greek translation of the Hebrew Bible, called the "Septuagint." Considering this, it is only natural that Luke's stories about Jesus—as well as those in Acts

concerning the early Church—connect, allude to, and echo the stories of the Old Testament. Luke is probably writing after the fall of Jerusalem in AD 70, and since almost all of Mark's Gospel is incorporated into Luke's account, it most likely followed the compilation of Mark as well.

> The Exile scattered the Jews to a number of surrounding areas outside Palestine. Since most of these Jews remained in their new homes, those who managed later to return to their native country were downtrodden to find themselves in the minority. Eventually, those Jews who lived beyond Palestine's borders came to be known as Jews of the Dispersion, or the Diaspora (Trafton, 477).

Studying

One thing is certain: Luke gives us *all* the names. Because of his dedication to this particular element, we know the names of John's father and mother: Zechariah and Elizabeth. Also because of Luke, we know that Zechariah's priestly order was Abijah and Elizabeth's was Aaron. Likewise, we know the name of the earthly Judean king who ruled during this time: Herod, whose son, Herod Antipas, would both kill John and aid in the onslaught of Jesus' torture and subsequent death. In fact, this is the same Herod who would be stricken by an angel for not giving glory to God (Acts 12:23).

> On an appointed day Herod put on his royal robes, took his seat on the platform, and delivered a public address to them. The people kept shouting, "The voice of a god, and not of a mortal!" And immediately, because he had not given the glory to God, an angel of the Lord struck him down, and he was eaten by worms and died. (Acts 12:21-23)

If the first readers of Luke's Gospel were familiar with the stories of God and Israel contained in the Hebrew Bible, then likely the description of Elizabeth and Zechariah would have reminded them of other previously barren couples: Sarai and Abram (Gen 18), Rebecca and Isaac (Gen 25), Rachel and Jacob (Gen 30), and Hannah and Elkanah (1 Sam 1-2). In each case, God used the most unexpected person to bring about God's surprising but delightful purposes. With Sarai, the promise was planted as a seed. Then, it was nurtured in Rebecca and later in Rachel. This same promise went on to flower into the kingship of David, beginning with Hannah. And now, with the announcement of the newborn Messiah, the promise begins to bear fruit.

Being childless was considered a curse in first-century Palestine. After all, children were considered a sign of God's blessing, and for older couples, of security. Even today, many couples who are not childless by choice report feeling less like a family. In addition, many of these individuals acknowledge being deeply saddened by their situation. Luke notes that Elizabeth and Zechariah "lived blamelessly according to all the command-ments" (1:6), which is particularly intriguing since no one else is ever deemed "blameless" in Luke or Acts.

Luke's story begins in the Temple in Jerusalem, picking up as the gospel is being announced to the Jews in the Holy of Holies in the Jerusalem Temple. Ultimately, his story will end with Paul preaching in prison in the court of Caesar in Rome (Acts 28). Although preached first to the Jews, the gospel is intended to be heard by *all* nations, implied by the fact that it starts in Jerusalem and spreads out like an exploding supernova.

Zechariah's name means "Yahweh has remembered," which works on at least two levels. First, God has remembered faithful Zechariah and his wife Elizabeth, whose name means "God's oath." Even in their old age, they will not be forgotten, but instead, will become parents. *And,* their son will be remarkable, the best and last of the prophets ever to precede the coming of the Messiah. Secondly, God has remembered the Jews, God's chosen people, and so God brings the announcement of the Messiah's impending arrival first to them. Yet, shattering any preconceived notions they may have had, this Jewish Messiah would be for all people everywhere. So for both the couple in this passage and the Jewish people, God has kept a promise.

Although he and his wife lived in the hill country (1:39), Zechariah was a priest in the Temple in Jerusalem. Since both he and Elizabeth were descendents of Aaron, he was entitled to serve in the Temple twice a year. Temple priests were split into 24 divi-sions, each named for one of Aaron's 24 sons (1 Chr 24:1-19). Priests typically served for two weeks a year. Within each group, the priest cast lots to decide who would officiate. The chosen priest would enter the inner sanctuary, offer the sacrifice, and burn incense. The burning incense represented the prayers of the people who stood outside and waited. It was the highest honor a priest could receive, especially since no priest was allowed to do it more than once in a lifetime.

As a matter of fact, it was at this very moment—the highest point of Zechariah's priestly career—that the unexpected happened: a messenger from God appeared. When Zechariah saw the angel, "he was terrified and fear overwhelmed him" (1:12), a common reaction of biblical characters to the sight of God's messengers. Repeatedly throughout Scripture, people are rendered deeply afraid when they encounter an angel (for example, 1:30; 2:10; 5:10; 8:50; Acts 18:9; 27:24; Gen 15:1; Dan 10:12; Isa 6:5-6). In light of this, we can only conclude that surely there must be something about an angel's presence that manages to penetrate human pretense.

The word "angel" is derived from the Greek word *angelos*, which means "messenger."

The angel in the passage offers two pieces of news. First, God has heard the couple's prayers and has promised them a son, who will be like the prophet Samuel (1 Sam 1:9-11). Like Samson (Judg 13:4) and Samuel (1 Sam 1:11) alike, this boy will be a child of promise, so he is required to abstain from drinking alcohol. Better yet, God will use him to call God's people back to God: "He will turn many people to the Lord their God" (1:16). This means, of course, that many of God's people were not yet turned toward their God: *I will send the prophet Elijah...He will turn the hearts of the parents to their children, and the hearts of the children to their parents.*

In other words, the old couple wouldn't bear just any son, but a son who would "make ready a people prepared for the Lord" (1:18)—the herald of God's Messiah! These two things are surely beyond Zechariah's wildest dreams. In one moment—again, the highest of his priestly career—he receives the news he has most longed for all his life: that he will have a son *and* the Messiah is coming soon!

Upon first hearing the joyful news, Zechariah is skeptical, insistent that the whole scenario sounds way too good to be true. So in a way, he tells the angel, "Oh yeah? Let me see some ID." It is possible that Zechariah had never expected God to speak, nor had he expected God to answer his and Elizabeth's yearning for a child. He also probably had not expected to hear that the Messiah, the promised and longed-for one, was coming soon. Quoting Genesis 15:8, Zechariah's response is like that of so many religious people in the Gospel of Luke and Acts. Many will react to the good news as Mary did, accepting it with pure, unadulterated wonder. Many others, however, will react like Zechariah, with sheer skepticism: *How will I know that this is so?*

Clearly, the angel in this lesson's narrative is indignant, so indignant in fact, that he strikes Zechariah mute! Surely, Gabriel felt that Zechariah's response undermined the very good news he received, but still, muteness must have been hard punishment for Zechariah to bear. After all, he had outrageously good news to share, but he could not speak it—no matter how hard he tried! Zechariah went out to the people, but could not tell them what he saw and heard. Before long, Elizabeth became pregnant, and went into seclusion soon after. This first story of Luke's Gospel ends with Zechariah speechless and Elizabeth sequestered. The suspense builds as we wonder what will happen next in this wild story of God's making good on divine promises.

Understanding

No doubt, Zechariah and his wife had prayed fervently for a child for quite a while. But, upon receiving the news that their prayers had been heard and answered, Zechariah's initial reaction was to be incredulous and suspicious. Clearly, he did not remember the famous stories of his own people, for if he had recalled the story of Abram and Sarai, for example, he would have remembered that giving children to an older couple is not difficult for God. Presented with news that is beyond his wildest dreams, Zechariah is unable to understand the easy part of the circumstances.

Often we are like Zechariah. When something we have fervently prayed and hoped for has come to pass, how do we tend to react? Too often we respond with disbelief and suspicion. If God were to grant us our deepest hopes, what would those be? If God sent to you a messenger, what good tidings might that messenger have to relay? Why do God's people have such trouble believing and accepting God's blessing?

Zechariah hears the word he has most longed to hear—and then some! Not only will he have a child, but this extraordinary child also will serve as the herald of God's chosen one. Surely, the news must have turned Zechariah's world on its end, and yet, his reaction is so typical of many of us. When confronted with the extraordinary, all we want to know is whether there are any strings attached. "What's the catch to all these blessings?" we want to know. "Can I get this in writing, Lord?" Can we not see how insulting such an attitude is to God's messengers?

What About Me?

• *God remembers.* God hears our prayers and never forgets that we are God's people. Even when we truly feel as though God has forgotten us, this simply is not so. Like Zechariah, maybe our plans for our lives are not "wild" enough. Perhaps our expectations of God are too tame, too safe.

• *As you worship, expect a message from God.* Zechariah was leading worship, but he never expected a message from God. This is entirely reminiscent of many of us who show up for worship, but never expect to hear a word from God, either in the Scripture reading, the music, or the moments of silence.

• *It is painful not to be able to share good news.* Zechariah found out that when a person does not believe in God's good news, it becomes impossible to share it with them. Always guard against taking for granted the joy and grace that comes from telling the good news.

• *Those who say they cherish the stories of God must make sure they know them and live them out.* Zechariah was a priest, the one most honored in his day, yet his response to the angel's message shows that he had forgotten the stories of the men and women of the Old Testament. All of us know people who are remark-ably well-versed in the Bible, but are so mean in their words and actions that they make it very apparent they know little about actually following Jesus. Each Christian needs to be wary of this danger. After having Bibles in our houses does not necessarily mean that we read them or live out the messages contained inside.

Resources

Raymond Brown, *The Birth of the Messiah* (Garden City NY: Doubleday, 1978).

Fred Craddock, *Luke* (Louisville: John Knox Press, 1990).

R. Alan Culpepper, "Luke," *New Interpreter's Bible*, vol. 9 (Nashville: Abingdon Press, 1995).

Earle E. Ellis, *The Gospel of Luke*, from The New Century Bible Commentary series (Grand Rapids: Eerdmans, 1974).

Craig A. Evans, *Luke*, from the New International Biblical Commentary series (Peabody MA: Hendrickson, 1990).

Joseph A. Fitzmyer, *The Gospel According to Luke* (I-IX), in Anchor Bible, vol. 28A (Garden City NY: Doubleday, 1983).

Luke Timothy Johnson, *The Gospel of Luke*, in Sacra Pagina, vol. 3 (Collegeville MN: Liturgical Press, 1991).

David L. Tiede, *Luke*, from Augsburg Commentary on the New Testament (Minneapolis: Augsburg, 1988).

Joseph L. Trafton, "Judaism," *Mercer Dictionary of the Bible*, ed. Watson E. Mills et al. (Macon: Mercer University Press, 1990).

HUSHED
BY AN ANGEL
Luke 1:5-25

Introduction

All our studies in this unit will concentrate on Luke, my favorite of all the Gospels. Mark is so direct and brief, while Matthew is so detailed. And even though John is wonderful, often I struggle to understand. Luke, on the other hand, does it all: tells unforgettable stories (like the Good Samaritan, the Prodigal Son/Elder Brother, and the Road to Emmaus), identifies with hurting people, even elevates women. Luke is also a very inclusive Gospel—even from the very start.

Zechariah was the father of John the Baptizer. In fact, were he not the father of John the Baptizer, we might never have heard of him. Luke's Gospel opens, telling about the miraculous birth of John the Baptizer, who not only would baptize Jesus but would also introduce him to a larger Jewish audience. As it happens, the nearer we get to Jesus, the more important the players in this story become. So, the question remains: are we to place the most emphasis on John the Baptizer or on Zechariah? Personally, I believe John should be our focus, especially since he was much closer to Jesus—who is the centerpiece of the New Testament—than his father.

The New Testament interrupts a long God-silence. When we enter the text, there has been no prophet in the land for several hundred years. What once had been so rich and full when Elijah, Amos, Isaiah, Micah, Ezekiel, and Jeremiah spoke is gone. Most Jews were into money, politics, and family life much more so than they were into religion. But John the Baptizer would change all that. So powerful was his message, so radical was his lifestyle, so fearless was his courage, until huge crowds couldn't help but be magnetized to him. So, what we want to know is: just how does a "John the Baptizer" come to be? What makes a prophet? Our own prophetless society needs to know these answers.

Out of the Best of Judaism, 1:5-10.

"There was a priest named Zechariah, who belonged to the priestly order of Abijah. His wife was a descendant of Aaron, and her name was Elizabeth. Both of them were righteous before God, living blamelessly according to all the commandments and regulations of the Lord" (Lk 1: 5-6). It seems as though God searched all over Judea to find the most godly, devout couple in the land, by whom God would raise up the prophet John the Baptist. Read further and Luke leads us to yet another couple, Mary and Joseph (1:26-38), who appear to be cut from the same cloth as Elizabeth and Zechariah.

It is stylish these days in media circles to highlight goodness in unexpected people. While this is a positive image, church people are often portrayed as the villains who turn away the help-less, whose only choice is to get help from individuals who make no pretense of religion. The messages are clear: bad people aren't as bad as we've made them out to be, and religious people often look more like pagans.

Luke, however, leads us in a different direction. "God is at work from within, not from outside the institutions, rituals, and practices of Judaism" (Fred Craddock, "Luke/John," *Interpretation*, A Bible Commentary, Louisville: Knox Press, 1990, 26). No one would have more trouble with organized religion than Jesus. Pharisees, chief priests, Sadduccees—these are the unrelenting "bad guys" in the Gospels. The people at the top were insensitive to the direction God was moving; the people at the bottom, on the other hand, were godly, constantly listening for a word from God.

Times haven't changed much. Many alleged "religious author-ities" today often are not terribly religious at all; rather, they tend to be "power people." But usually those at the bottom, those who teach our children about Jesus, sing in the choir, and usher at church—these are servant people. John the Baptist emerged from *within* Judaism to become a severe critic of the same system that produced him.

Out of Godly Desire, 1:7 and 13.

"But they had no children, because Elizabeth was barren, and both were getting on in years...The angel said to him, 'Do not be afraid, Zechariah, for your prayer has been heard'" (1:7 and 13). I doubt any of us can fully recreate the emptiness a Jewish couple felt when they were childless. After all, they had no science to help them understand their predicament, and in the meantime, the culture placed blame for childlessness on the woman. Abraham and Sarah, Elkanah and Hannah, were childless couples of the Old Testament, but it was the women who were made to feel like failures.

"Jewish Rabbis said that seven people were excommunicated from God and the list began, 'A Jew who has no wife, or a Jew who has a wife and who has no child.' Childlessness was a valid ground for divorce" (William Barclay, *The Gospel of Luke*, Philadelphia: Westminster Press, 1956, 4). A sure sign that romantic love was just as alive in biblical times as it is now is the dedication some men showed to their barren wives. Yet, even though many of them did not see this as grounds for casting away their beloved spouses, that did not take away the sting of childlessness. Whereas men felt cheated, women felt the judgment of a society that expected children.

Without a doubt, John the Baptizer was a wanted child. Even though the stilted language of Luke masks Elizabeth's sheer elation, neither centuries nor culture can hide her joy. Too old to have a child, Elizabeth knew that God had to figure into the equation somewhere. "This is what the Lord has done for me when he looked favorably on me and took away the disgrace I have endured among my people" (1:25). John was not just another mouth to feed; John was a gift from God. Besides, a wanted child has an advantage from the start. To never wonder if you are loved, to never wonder if your parents have time for you, to never wonder whether you are going to church, to never wonder if your parents are what they say they are—these securities give identity. To be wanted is life's first blessing.

Out of a Disciplined Self-Denial, 1:15-16.

"You will have joy and gladness, and many will rejoice at his birth, for he will be great in the sight of the Lord. He must never drink wine or strong drink; even before his birth he will be filled with the Holy Spirit. He will turn many of the people of Israel to the Lord their God" (1:14-16). John the Baptizer was not born to be the warm, cuddly baby that turns every grandmother's head. John was born for stern stuff. Most commentators make no mention of the passage "He must never drink wine or strong drink; even before birth he will be filled with the Holy Spirit" (1:15). I think that we cannot fully understand John the Baptizer unless we recognize the self-denial that was built into him from before his birth.

Walter Russell Bowie wrote of John, "He was clothed with the awful moral authority which belongs only to those who have yielded themselves to be instruments of God. In him men saw again the power which had been in Elijah, Amos, and Isaiah..." (*The Compassionate Christ*, New York: Abingdon Press, 1965, 18). The angel's prediction of the kind of person John would be was quickly confirmed (Lk 3:1-20). He didn't dress like other people; in fact, he was quite plain. Likewise, he didn't live in Jerusalem or Caesarea where important people lived; instead, he made his pulpit in the Judean wilderness. In fact, he even ate a peculiar diet of "locusts and wild honey" (Mt 3:4). In modern language, we might say that John was "a character." But that's not all there was to John.

Unlike those preachers who pretend to be prophets, John was more interested in truth than public opinion. "John said to the crowds that came out to be baptized by him, 'You brood of vipers! Who warned you to flee from the wrath to come?...Even now the ax is lying at the root of the trees; every tree therefore that does not bear good fruit is cut down and thrown into the fire" (Lk 3:7-9). How do you get to be tough enough, honest enough, bold enough to speak the truth? Even from his birth, John was reared to stand alone, to be different, to have a moral edge.

John was under the severe discipline that goes with a special vow unto the Lord. The key words are these: "When men or women make a special vow, the vow of a nazirite, to separate themselves to the Lord, they shall separate themselves from wine and strong drink...No razor shall come upon the head...they shall be holy..." (Num 6:2-5). These days, we hear very little about special vows, holiness, self-denial, rigor, and discipline . We, of course, are more prone to "feel-good religion," but John was much different from us. Too many John the Baptists running around could ruin a church picnic. After all, there is no record that he had any semblance of a sense of humor. But what he did have were scruples. People came to him because he didn't negotiate moral truth; he *lived* it.

Out of the Intention of God, 1:15, 17.

"You will have joy and gladness, and many will rejoice at his birth, for he will be great in the sight of the Lord...With the spirit and power of Elijah he will go before him, to turn the hearts of parents to their children, and the disobedient to the wisdom of the righteous, to make ready a people prepared for the Lord" (1:15, 17). Clearly, we have lots of key phrases imbedded into this passage:

(1) "He will be great in the sight of the Lord..." (1:15a). John was meant to be different, and he succeeded. Because he was such a pest—and more accurately, a threat—to the religious establishment, they kept their eye on him. John is kept for us in the Bible because he was "great in the sight of the Lord."

(2) "With the spirit and power of Elijah he will go before him..." (1:17a). Often John the Baptizer has been called the "forerunner," for he was sent before Jesus to prepare people for the coming of the Messiah. The reason Luke begins his "life of Christ" with John is because John the Baptizer was an integral piece in God's design. John's baptism of repentance was not God's last word, but it was a step in the right direction, a sort of "get ready" for the message Jesus would bring.

(3) "He will go before him...to make ready a people prepared for the Lord" (1:17). Baptism and temptations were first. Then "Jesus came to Galilee, proclaiming the good news of God, and saying, 'The time is fulfilled, and the kingdom of God has come

near; repent, and believe in the good news'" (Mk 1:14-15). This was the opening, the very beginning of Jesus' public ministry. But Jesus did not just come out of nowhere. He built his ministry on the work of John. Crowds of people had flocked to John; now many of those same people couldn't get enough of Jesus.

Zechariah and Elizabeth performed valuable service. They gave a son who prepared the way not only for a Savior but for us all. Granted, Zechariah had a faith failure and was made mute for a time, but that's a small factor in the grand scheme of things. Take the long look. See the forest, not the brush. We know about this devout couple because they reared the prophet who paved the way for Jesus. And in the meantime, John's moral edge cost him his head. Living on the moral edge is always expensive—both then and now.

Notes

Notes

2

JUST SAY
YES

Luke 1:26-38

Central Question

When God calls, will we dare to say yes?

Scripture

Luke 1:26-38 In the sixth month the angel Gabriel was sent by God to a town in Galilee called Nazareth, 27 to a virgin engaged to a man whose name was Joseph, of the house of David. The virgin's name was Mary. 28 And he came to her and said, "Greetings, favored one! The Lord is with you." 29 But she was much perplexed by his words and pondered what sort of greeting this might be. 30 The angel said to her, "Do not be afraid, Mary, for you have found favor with God. 31 And now, you will conceive in your womb and bear a son, and you will name him Jesus. 32 He will be great, and will be called the Son of the Most High, and the Lord God will give to him the throne of his ancestor David. 33 He will reign over the house of Jacob forever, and of his kingdom there will be no end." 34 Mary said to the angel, "How can this be, since I am a virgin?" 35 The angel said to her, "The Holy Spirit will come upon you, and the power of the Most High will overshadow you; therefore the child to be born will be holy; he will be called Son of God. 36 And now, your relative Elizabeth in her old age has also conceived a son; and this is the sixth month for her who was said to be barren. 37 For nothing will be impossible with God." 38 Then Mary said, "Here am I, the servant of the Lord; let it be with me according to your word." Then the angel departed from her.

Remembering

Luke begins his Gospel by announcing the birth of a new "Elijah," the forerunner to the Messiah. To be a bit more specific, Gabriel is the divine messenger who makes this remarkable announcement to a priest in the inner sanctuary of the Temple. So, Gabriel—the "right" messenger—delivered the news of

> "With the spirit and power of Elijah he will go before him, to turn the hearts of parents to their children, and the disobedient to the wisdom of the righteous, to make ready a people prepared for the Lord." (Lk 1:17)

incredible joy to Zechariah—the "right" person—during Israel's occupation by the Romans—the "right" time—in the sacred space of the Temple—the "right" place. And to be sure, the news itself was even "right-er" than all the other factors which seemed to fall so beautifully into place.

However, despite all this, Gabriel's triumphant message was received in exactly the *wrong* way, greeted by nothing more than Zechariah's sheer skepticism and silence: *How do I know this is true, since my wife and I are old?* Remarkably, the priest seemed to have completely forgotten about similar episodes that had gone on

> Zechariah should have been quite familiar with the stories of Sarai and Abraham, of Rebecca and Isaac, of Rachel and Jacob, and of Hannah and Elkanah—all older couples who, like Zechariah himself, were surprised by the unexpected news that children were in their midst.

before Zechariah and his wife. After all, this was not the first time Yahweh had blessed an older barren couple with a child.

Because Zechariah met the amazing news with a closed mind, he would also have to endure his mouth being closed as well. For his skepticism, Gabriel struck Zechariah mute until his son's birth. As you can see, the first scene of Luke's Gospel ends on a less-than-positive note. Zechariah is forced into silence, and meanwhile, Elizabeth is pregnant and in seclusion. What will happen next? Will the announcement of the Messiah's birth warrant more joy than this?

Studying

Clearly, Luke loves drawing parallels between stories with contrasting characters. For instance, in the stories of John and Jesus, notice these parallel themes: both involve announcements to faithful Jews of a miraculous birth, both are set in motion by God, both concern the Messiah, and both are reminiscent of Sarah and Abraham's situation. Most notably, in this lesson's passage both the elderly couple and the unmarried young woman are extremely unlikely candidates for giving birth. As God has consistently proven, some of the most improbable people can play significant roles in bringing about the Kingdom. In addition, both stories follow the same angelic progression: Gabriel arrives and commands his hearer not to be afraid; he delivers his joyful message, which is received with some doubt; the angel answers questions and leaves.

Stories involving angels who speak are called *angelophany*.

However, even though Zechariah and Elizabeth's circumstances certainly resemble Mary's, the main characters nevertheless stand in sharp contrast to each other. For example, Gabriel, who first visited a man, now visits a girl. Besides that, keep in mind that the first message was delivered at the holiest place in all of Jerusalem—so holy, in fact, that it was called the Holy City. Now, however, the message graces one of the poorer regions of Palestine, the backwater town of southern Galilee. And by the same token, Elizabeth and her husband are married, while Mary was merely engaged. Zechariah is older; Mary is young, likely between the ages of 12 and 16. Zechariah answered Gabriel with skepticism; Mary answers with utter astonishment.

Some might wonder how Gabriel felt during the six-month span between the announcement of John's coming birth and this one to Mary. Might he have thought to himself, "If an experienced, learned priest couldn't help being suspicious, how could I *possibly* expect a young girl to receive this unbelievable news?" In *Peculiar Treasures*, Frederick Buechner makes the following remarks about Gabriel's announcement to Mary:

She [Mary] struck the angel Gabriel as hardly old enough to have a child at all, let alone this child, but he's been entrusted with a message to give her, and he gave it.... "You mustn't be afraid, Mary," he said. As he said it, he only hoped she wouldn't notice that beneath the great, golden wings he himself was trembling with fear to think that the whole future of creation hung now on the answer of a girl. (39)

Sent by God, the divine messenger comes to Mary with these words: *Greetings, favored one! The Lord is with you* (Lk 1:28). As to be expected, Mary does not know what to make of the angel's remarks. How was she favored—by whom and why? How is it that God is with *her*, of all people? Understandably, she is perplexed; in fact, the Greek goes so far as to say that "she was deeply disturbed." But then again, if an angel of God appeared to us with such affirming words, how would we react?

> A few Greek manuscripts of this particular Gospel borrow from verse 42, adding this phrase to Gabriel's greeting: "Blessed are you among women."

Keeping with the tradition of other famous angels, Gabriel adds, "Do not be afraid" (1:30). Obviously, there is something about the appearance of divine messengers that serves to strike fear in even the best of us. Hoping to avoid this typical response, however, the good news tumbles out of Gabriel before Mary has time to comprehend what is going on:

You have found favor with God (v. 30);
You will conceive and bear a son (v. 31);
His name will be Jesus (a form of "Joshua," meaning *salvation*);
He will be called the son of the Most High (v. 32);
The Lord God will give to him the throne of his ancestor David (v. 32);
He will reign over the house of Jacob forever (v. 33);
Of his kingdom, there will be no end (v. 33).

This would have been quite a lot for *anyone* to have taken in, let alone a person as young as Mary. This child was to be the Son of God. He was to be a king whose dominion would have no end. With promises so enormous, how could Mary have understood it all?

In regard to why Mary was chosen, the text reveals only that she had "found favor with God." Apparently, God had taken note of the faithfulness of this young woman. It was her past allegiance that made possible her future responsibility: the difficult chore and amazing call to give birth to God's only child.

As we find to be the case with Zechariah, the angel's announcement of good news here is met with a question: "How can this be, since I am a virgin?" (1:34). In Gabriel's eyes, Mary's question is legitimate—perhaps because in her situation there is no historical parallel to God's actions. But as far as he is concerned, Zechariah should have known better. A virgin conceiving, however, was a new thing altogether. So Gabriel explains further, again with a litany of extraordinary events:

> The Holy Spirit will come upon you.
> The power of the Most High will overshadow you.
> The child to be born will be holy.
> He will be called Son of God.
> Your relative Elizabeth in her old age has also conceived a son. (1:36)

Never at a loss for words, Gabriel keeps listing the blessings that will abound from this precious experience, blessings that sound too good to be true. Overshadowed by the Most High and covered by the Holy Spirit, Mary will conceive and give birth to God's son. As she tries desperately to soak all this in, Gabriel can only hint at the enormity of this adventure and the outrageousness of this promise.

Reminiscent of God's words to Abraham and Sarai from Genesis 18:14—"Is anything too wonderful for the Lord?"— Gabriel offers this observation: "For nothing will be impossible to God." As far as one-sentence summaries go, this is a particularly good one for the entire Bible. Indeed, the entire story of salvation is filled with evidence revealing that *nothing* is impossible to God.

Finally, to add to the intensity of the account, a 14-year-old utters some of the most exceptional words of trust in all of Scripture: *Here am I, the servant of the Lord; let it be with me according to your word* (1:38). Although she does not fully understand the angel's message, Mary places her absolute trust in God. Without a further word, Gabriel departs.

Understanding

As we review Mary's story, keep sight of one detail: Mary had a choice. She could have chosen simply to refuse the great honor offered to her. Yet, as John Claypool remarks, "God proposed, and Mary seconded the motion." God does not force the divine will on anyone; instead, God calls and invites. We can always opt to neglect God's call. We can even refuse God and, in fact, many of us do so every day.

What if Mary *had* turned down God's offer? Would the Messiah have been born to another Jewish girl, or perhaps in a different place and time altogether? Naturally, we can only speculate, for the birth, gender, place, and ethnic identity of God's chosen one is shrouded in the mystery of God's will and purposes. Even so, we have to wonder whether Mary was the first woman to whom God ever made this proposition. As outlandish as it might seem, imagine for a moment that there had been another woman who said quite simply, "No thanks." What if, in the six months between the announcement of John's birth and this one to Mary, Gabriel had been turned down? Of course, whether Mary was the first or not, the important thing is that she was the last. Mary was more than willing to make her contribution to God's plan. God needs more people to risk a "yes" in the name of the Messiah.

By contrasting Zechariah and Mary, Luke wants his readers to discover at least two different ways of greeting the news of the Messiah's coming: either with skepticism and suspicion or with openness and joy. Luke would rather we be more like Mary—and less like Zechariah—receiving God's good news with nothing less than pure delight.

What About Me?

• *We can choose to say either yes or no to God.* God doesn't force anyone into servitude. Rather, God offers and invites. We can choose either to accept the blessing and hard work or to watch from the sidelines.

- *Mary's son would bring her both great honor and tremendous pain.* When Mary agreed to become the mother of the Christ child, she had no clue as to how the story would unfold. There would be times when she was proud of her son, but also times when she would not understand him at all. Then finally, she would grieve his death, becoming a disciple of her own child, the son of the Most High (Acts 1).

- *We may greet the gospel with either suspicion or surrender.* Often the good news of God is so incredible that it is hard to believe. In these days, we do not believe many things very easily. In this way, we are more akin to Zechariah than Mary, though we should strive to accept the gospel with Mary's sense of surrender to God.

- *We need to remember that God often uses young people.* Mary was probably 16 years old at most, yet God chose her to bear and raise Jesus. Throughout history, God has often used young people to revive the Church. In fact, every major Christian revival in America has started with young people. Christians need to remember that youth are our future and are capable of accomplishing great things for God. If we are wise, we dare not underestimate them or their priceless contributions.

Resources

Raymond Brown, *The Birth of the Messiah* (Garden City NY: Doubleday, 1978).

Fred Craddock, *Luke* (Louisville: John Knox Press, 1990).

R. Alan Culpepper, "Luke," *New Interpreter's Bible*, vol. 9 (Nashville: Abingdon Press, 1995).

Earle E. Ellis, *The Gospel of Luke*, from The New Century Bible Commentary series (Grand Rapids: Eerdmans, 1974).

Craig A. Evans, *Luke*, from the New International Biblical Commentary series (Peabody MA: Hendrickson, 1990).

Joseph A. Fitzmyer, *The Gospel According to Luke* (I-IX), in Anchor Bible, vol. 28A (Garden City NY: Doubleday, 1983).

Luke Timothy Johnson, *The Gospel of Luke*, in Sacra Pagina, vol. 3 (Collegeville MN: Liturgical Press, 1991).

David L. Tiede, *Luke*, from Augsburg Commentary on the New Testament (Minneapolis: Augsburg, 1988).

JUST SAY YES

Luke 1:26-38

Introduction

Last lesson we moved toward "Jesus' Birth" by looking at John the Baptizer, a key player in the design of God that led to Jesus. This lesson our text moves a step closer, as Mary, the mother of Jesus, becomes the new focus of our study. Mary is a bit of a mystery to Protestants. In fact, where Catholics have been very vocal and deliberate about Mary's place in biblical history, Protestants have been just as silent. Maybe Catholics have said too much and we've said too little. Regardless, this session helps us think about who she was, what God asked of her, and how she responded to God's calling. This much is certain: Mary had more to do with the formation of Jesus' character than anyone else— short of God, of course. And while the Scriptural base for our study is slim, it certainly is worth our best effort. Besides, Luke is a careful writer, not to mention liberal with details.

(1) "In the sixth month...," means it had been six months since Elizabeth's conception of John the Baptist.

(2) Gabriel was God's messenger (as implied by the fact that "angel" literally means "messenger"), and in Luke angels appear often.

(3) Mary lived in Nazareth, a small town in southern Galilee with a poor reputation (see Jn 1:46).

(4) Mary was engaged to Joseph. Engagement typically lasted a year and was considered unconditionally binding. To break an engagement required a divorce. Joseph's name is mentioned in our text, although no specific details are offered (1:27). Neither do we have any details surrounding Mary's age, but commentators

agree unanimously that she was young (that is, by our standards for "marrying age"), maybe somewhere between 14 and 16 years old.

(5) Clearly, God took the lead in this text. Mary did not ask for Gabriel; she did not seek special assignment from God. "In the sixth month the angel Gabriel was sent by God...to a virgin engaged..." (1:26-27). Mary was minding her own business when her life suddenly was interrupted by a visitor from God. But as we know, God has been doing things like that for a long time.

The Favor of God, 1:28-30.

"And he came to her and said, 'Greetings, favored one! The Lord is with you'" (1:28). Mary didn't know what to make of Gabriel—or his greeting, for that matter. "She was much perplexed by his words and pondered what sort of greeting this might be. The angel said to her, 'Do not be afraid, Mary, for you have found favor with God'" (1:29-30). Most of us want to find "favor with God," and we tend to assume that if we are pleasing to God, then we will be rewarded with a perfect life. We can only speculate at best as to what Mary thought of her revered status in the eyes of God, but we do know what it meant in the years that stretched before her.

• Nine months later she would make a difficult trip to Bethlehem, separated from everything familiar and soon to give birth in a stable. That she was "favored of God" did not mean her life would be easy.
• As she watched Jesus grow up, surely she must have discerned in him a sense of greatness, and perhaps even more importantly, a sense of mission. And as every parent can understand, he just seemed to grow up too soon. Soon he was under fire from Pharisees and priests. Mary felt the tension and must have feared for her boy. "Favored of God" was heavy.
• Once while Jesus was visiting the synagogue at Nazareth, he was asked to read from the scrolls and offer some remarks. What he said angered the home folks so much that they actually ran him out of town—all while Mary stood by and watched.

• Accompanied by Jesus' brothers, Mary went to Capernaum to persuade her outcast son to come home. But not surprisingly, he would not. Mary knew all too well that Jesus was headed straight for trouble.

• Finally, the road led to Jerusalem and three crosses on a hill, where Mary watched as a part of her died, trying to remember that it was all a part of being "favored of God."

Walter Russell Bowie develops this idea further: "She was linked with the life of Jesus. As she had been part of all his sorrows, she would be part of his spiritual triumph too" (*The Compassionate Christ*, New York: Abingdon Press, 1965, 22). To be favored of God meant hard assignment. Individuals such as Moses and the Apostle Paul, for example, could identify with this more closely than they may have liked. Everybody wants leadership and fame, but we have to understand that God does not call us to ease through life. Quite to the contrary, God calls us "to enter into life profoundly" (Ibid.). We study Mary because her life was joined to Jesus, and thus, had extraordinary meaning because of it. After all, isn't that what being "favored" is all about?

A Request from God, 1:31-33.

"And now, you will conceive in your womb and bear a son, and you will name him Jesus. He will be great, and will be called the Son of the Most High, and the Lord God will give to him the throne of his ancestor David. He will reign over the house of Jacob forever..." (1:31-33). The way the language reads, it appears as though Gabriel was telling Mary what she *had* to do. But that simply wasn't the case. Mary had a choice. In fact, verse 38 would not be in the Bible in the first place had she not had a choice.

Parts of the Bible we can understand because the subject matter is close to our own experience. But if you're like me, you can't even begin to fathom what went through Mary's mind when Gabriel asked her to bear Jesus. Yet, one aspect of our text we do understand is that God *still* asks certain people to take on special assignments.

One of the courses I taught in seminary was titled "The Life and Work of the Pastor," during which I tried to help my students prepare for lives of ministry. There is no sugar-coating the profession, nor is there any accurate prediction of how tough it's going to be. I told my classes with utter sincerity that there would be good times and bad times. If they didn't truly feel called to the work, they were bound to get into trouble. However, if they really believed that God wanted them to be pastors, God would help them find a way. Nobody *has* to devote their life to ministry. It is a thing we either consent or flat-out refuse to do. In fact, when I was a boy, the language was "*surrender* to preach"!

God doesn't force unwilling participants to work for the Kingdom, but even now God is *still* asking believers to take on special assignments. Sadly, some of the most able turn away from God's call to service and go their own way instead. Mary became immortal because she aligned her little life with the enormous purposes of God.

The Ways of God, 1:34-37.

"Mary said to the angel, 'How can this be, since I am a virgin?' The angel said to her, 'The Holy Spirit will come upon you, and the power of the Most High will overshadow you; therefore the child to be born will be holy; he will be called the Son of God...'" (1:34-35). Both Luke and Matthew (see Mt 1:18-25) tell of the "virgin birth," but strangely enough, it is never mentioned anywhere else in the New Testament. Sad to say, there has been very little study surrounding the virgin birth, yet it has become a measuring stick among many congregations. In other words, these individuals insist that if you believe in the virgin birth, then you also "believe the Bible." If you have questions about the virgin birth, however, you are deemed a liberal. So, where's the common ground?

(1) "How can this be, since I am a virgin?" When Zechariah questioned Gabriel, he was penalized (see 1:18). Mary's question, on the other hand, was given serious consideration, and she wasn't counted faithless just for asking. This gives me hope, for the ways of God sometimes raise questions in my own mind.

Surely, none of us ever means to offend God; we just want to know more.

(2) Jesus was a miracle. I have no trouble believing in the virgin birth. Jesus often violated what has come to be called natural law: he turned water into wine, he walked on water, he raised the dead. Plain and simple, miracles were a part of Jesus' daily routine. Where we go wrong is in making more of the virgin birth than does the New Testament itself.

(3) Was Mary demanding explanation before she would give consent? Following Jesus is faith-based. Christians do things that "make sense," of course, but this is certainly not the measure of all things. If you asked me to make sense of my love for my wife, I would be hard-pressed. In some ways Dot and I should never have married, but we "believed" in each other. The "believing" gets us past the "How can this be?" Christianity is not always the best explanation for life; in fact, it is *beyond* explanation. Mary couldn't possibly know how Jesus would be born or what would become of him, yet she believed anyway.

The Only Answer for God, 1:38.

"Then Mary said, 'Here am I, the servant of the Lord; let it be with me according to your word.' Then the angel departed from her" (1:38). If your class becomes bogged down in the whole idea of the "virgin birth" discussion, they could easily miss a full treatment of Mary's answer. In that case, they would miss the main theme of the passage altogether. Just face it: *nobody* can "explain" the virgin birth. You either believe it or you don't.

But Mary's answer was different. She was hardly more than a child, and Gabriel was asking her to do something that would raise a lot more than eyebrows. Naturally, we can be smug and claim that we would have done the same thing, but then again, we also read this text coached by two thousand years of Christian doctrine. Mary, on the other hand, was flying blindly. But that little Galilean girl became a teacher for us all.

(1) "Here am I, the servant of the Lord...," was Mary's answer. And she meant it. When I was a boy, the invitation hymn at

church was often B. B. McKinney's "Wherever He Leads I'll Go." The first verse is as follows:

"Take up thy cross and follow me,"
I heard my Master say;
"I gave my life to ransom thee,
Surrender your all today."

Wherever he leads I'll go,
Wherever he leads I'll go,
I'll follow my Christ who loves me so,
Wherever he leads I'll go.
(*The Baptist Hymnal*, Nashville: Convention Press, 1975, hymn #361)

Mary did exactly what McKinney's words ask of us all.

(2) "Let it be with me according to your word." Nothing was held back. Everything was released. Any semblance of control Mary had over her body, her life, her future—all was given, released, relinquished. She turned it over to God, even though she may not have fully understood what she was doing at the time. And just who was Mary? She was just a girl in a backwater town called Nazareth. But we study Mary because she said yes. Should God call on me, hopefully I could do the same as a scared teenage girl so many centuries ago.

Notes

Notes

3

LEAPING
FOR JOY
Luke 1:39-56

Central Question

How is God eliciting praise from you?

Scripture

Luke 1:39-56 In those days Mary set out and went with haste to a Judean town in the hill country, 40 where she entered the house of Zechariah and greeted Elizabeth. 41 When Elizabeth heard Mary's greeting, the child leaped in her womb. And Elizabeth was filled with the Holy Spirit 42 and exclaimed with a loud cry, "Blessed are you among women, and blessed is the fruit of your womb. 43 And why has this happened to me, that the mother of my Lord comes to me? 44 For as soon as I heard the sound of your greeting, the child in my womb leaped for joy. 45 And blessed is she who believed that there would be a fulfillment of what was spoken to her by the Lord." 46 And Mary said, "My soul magnifies the Lord, 47 and my spirit rejoices in God my Savior, 48 for he has looked with favor on the lowliness of his servant. Surely, from now on all generations will call me blessed; 49 for the Mighty One has done great things for me, and holy is his name. 50 His mercy is for those who fear him from generation to generation. 51 He has shown strength with his arm; he has scattered the proud in the thoughts of their hearts. 52 He has brought down the powerful from their thrones, and lifted up the lowly; 53 he has filled the hungry with good things, and sent the rich away empty. 54 He has helped his servant Israel, in remembrance of his mercy, 55 according to the promise he made

to our ancestors, to Abraham and to his descendants forever."
56 And Mary remained with her about three months and then
returned to her home.

Remembering

After addressing his Gospel to "most excellent Theophilus," a
reference either to one of our author's patrons or to anyone who
loves God, Luke goes on to describe two incidents involving visits
by the angel Gabriel. In the first of these accounts, the old priest
Zechariah is the recipient of the angel's message, which reveals
that his wife, Elizabeth, will soon bear a son. According to
Gabriel, the boy will become a remarkable man—"great in the
sight of the Lord" (1:15)—and in fact, will "turn many to the Lord
their God." (1:16) He will boast the spirit and power of Elijah,
echoing the promise of Malachi 4:5-6—and all this in order to
make a "people prepared for the Lord!" (1:18) In spite of the
angel's amazing news, however, Zechariah is skeptical, and as
"reward" for his suspicion, Gabriel strikes him mute until the
birth of his child.

Even more astounding is that six months later, Gabriel brings
a *second* announcement, except this time he proclaims a *divine*
birth, and this time the recipient is a young, unmarried Jewish
girl. Absolutely unable to comprehend how she could possibly be
the one chosen to bear the son of the Most High (1:32, 35), Mary's
first question is how she could be pregnant in the first place,
considering that she is still a virgin. But after hearing Gabriel's
careful explanation, she responds faithfully: *Here am I, the servant
of the Lord; let it be with me according to your word* (1:38).

Through his accounts of Zechariah and Mary, Luke holds up
for his readers two very different responses to God's call upon a
person's life: cautious skepticism and faithful obedience. In the
meantime, we find that in this lesson's passage he brings the two
storylines together, as Mary—who is with child—visits her relative
Elizabeth—also with child.

Studying

The angel departs, and likewise, so does Mary. She responds the way a person who has just received incredible news *should*: by running and telling it. As the Scripture notes, she "went with haste" to a town in the hill country, to Elizabeth and Zechariah's home. No doubt about it, this is a woman on a mission. When the two pregnant women greet each other, Elizabeth's unborn child surprises her with an unexpected kick. In fact, his sudden leap may be an echo of Rebekah's discomfort with the twin struggling within her in Genesis 25:22.

But of even more concern to us is what might be the intent of such an echo. Two ideas come to mind. First, Luke's grand scheme is to show how from the very beginning Jesus has been an essential element—*the* essential element—in God's perfect plan. In other words, Luke wants his audience to understand that redemption brought by the Messiah—who suffered, died, and was raised—has been God's sole intention all along. To be sure, the birth story of Jesus is a continuation of the salvation story that began in the Old Testament. Secondly, Luke may also be making a deliberate allusion to the story of Jacob and Esau, an account in which the older one serves the younger. After all, this will also be the story of John and Jesus, which is a further reminder that Jesus—*not* John—is the Messiah.

Scholars speculate that Luke is probably using the Greek translation of the Hebrew Bible called the "Septuagint," since many of his quotations seem to originate from this version rather than from the Hebrew directly. When it comes to matters like these, though, modern readers can only guess.

Clearly, Luke has quite a knack for telling a new story in such a way that it becomes reminiscent of an earlier one from the Old Testament. In his Gospel as well as Acts, Luke's words will remind the alert reader over and over again of earlier accounts in which God was a major working force. By cleverly incorporating this element of repetition into his work, Luke is implying that the story of Jesus, along with the call to carry the gospel to *all* people—including the Gentiles—have been primary factors in God's big plan all along.

Of particular interest is that Elizabeth is the first prophet ever mentioned in the book of Luke, and just as we find to be the case with Jesus in Matthew 5 and the seven blessings of the book of Revelation, she also gives blessings. The first of these was, "Blessed are you among women" (1:42a). Granted, Mary was blessed with being the mother of Jesus, but the fact that she gave birth to Jesus was not necessarily her destiny. In fact, the best thing Luke has to say about Mary has nothing at all to do with her role as Jesus' birth mother, but rather, with the fact that she eventually became one of his followers (see Acts 1:14). This point of view resurfaces in Luke 11:27, when a woman in the crowd says to Jesus, "Blessed is the womb that bore you, and the breasts that nursed you!," to which Jesus answers, "Blessed rather are those who hear the word of God and obey it!" (11:28)

> Repeatedly in Luke's two volumes, certain individuals will be *filled with the Holy Spirit* immediately before they say something of singular importance. Jesus, Peter, Paul, and many others—all are examples of such a phenomenon. The text tells us that Elizabeth was *filled with the Holy Spirit* (1:42), satisfying Gabriel's announcement to Zechariah, when the angel said to the priest, "Even before his birth he will be filled with the Holy Spirit." (1:15)

Elizabeth's second blessing follows quickly behind her first: "Blessed is the fruit of your womb" (1:42b). Having first blessed Mary, Elizabeth goes on to lift up the unborn Messiah as well. This is especially of interest considering that it is unlikely that Mary's pregnancy is already evident, not to mention that Luke never says anything about Mary's telling her cousin about the angel and the baby. And yet, Elizabeth *knows*—clued in perhaps by feeling the Holy Spirit envelop her in the presence of the woman who would conceive the Savior of us all.

The third blessing Elizabeth offered might have been intended for both Mary *and* Elizabeth herself: "And blessed is she who believed that there would be a fulfillment of what was spoken to her by the Lord" (1:45). Like the two midwives of Exodus, Shiphrah and Pu'ah, these two women helped safeguard the future of salvation. Mary came to Elizabeth of her own accord, proving both her firm belief in the angel's good news and her unconditional loyalty to God. After all, as is true in any case, authentic belief in God's Word is reflected through one's actions.

Notice that Elizabeth is the one who announces that "the child in my womb leaped for joy" (1:44). Gabriel had promised that she and her husband would delight and rejoice over this child, and it has come true even before his birth! At this point in the passage, Mary breaks into praise, an event termed as her "Magnificat," since that is the first word in the Latin translation of the text. Mary's song is significant for a number of reasons.

> Joy is one of the more pervasive themes in both Luke and Acts. A great personal Bible study would involve marking every mention of the word "joy" in both books, then summarizing Luke's assertions about this the most favored of all emotions—not to mention, the one held in common by those who believe in Christ.

First, the hymn is suggestive of Hannah's song, which was sung at Samuel's birth. In fact, in 1 Samuel 2:1-10, Hannah strikes many of the same chords that Mary will later on. For example, common themes in both hymns involve God's exaltation of the poor, God's bringing down the mighty, and of course, God's empowerment of the faithful. When Luke wants to depict Mary as the faithful, ideal mother, he adopts the same words and phrases that were used to describe Hannah. This is not to say that Luke "created" these stories about Mary. It *does* suggest, however, that he consciously told Mary's story in the language of Hannah's experience. Again, he does this to reinforce the continuation of the line from ancestor to descendant. By employing these devices to the advantage of the Kingdom, Luke is tugging on the sleeves of his readers, whispering, "The same God who gave Samuel to and through Hannah is now giving Jesus to and through Mary."

Second, Mary refers to God as *Savior* (1:47). Although Luke uses the term more than the other Gospel writers, even he does not use it much. Perhaps an even more notable characteristic of Mary's song, though, is its underlying implication that in relationship to the world's values, at first glance God's seem a bit upside-down. After all, consider: God brings down the powerful (1:53), sends "the rich away empty" (1:53), and has "scattered the proud" (1:51). God also has raised the lowly (1:48, 52), "filled the hungry with good things" (1:53), and given mercy to those who fear God (1:50). Like the psalms, Mary's hymn makes it clear that more often than not, God's values do not reflect those of the secular culture. God appraises people not by their status or financial situation, but by their hearts, their humility, and their faithfulness. Certainly this is one of the prevailing themes of all of Luke's writings.

Finally, a fourth important observation surrounding the Magnificat is that it speaks of God's saving actions as already accomplished. God has brought down, has shown strength, has filled the hungry, has helped Israel. Jesus' birth is not just a promise; it is a fulfillment. God has done all these things, and will continue to do them through the Messiah, Mary's son. God is active in all scenarios: past, present, *and* future.

Finally, the key verse in Mary's song is likely the last. In 1:55 Mary says that God does all this *according to the promise God made to our ancestors, to Abraham and his descendents forever.* God's actions to bring Jesus into the world are an extension of the promise God made to Abraham long ago. God keeps divine promises, and now the much awaited Messiah will come as Mary's child.

Understanding

Although it has been said many times, it still bears repeating: God uses the most unlikely people to accomplish God's purposes. Fortunately, Mary and Elizabeth recognized God's work and jumped with joy at the notion of taking part in the divine plan.

Too often we treat only the gifted and talented as special, and in the process, ignore the outcasts banished to the fringes of society. We would do well to remember that God has a soft spot for the poor, the hurting, the "one lost sheep." And if God uses the lowly, the hungry, and those who fear God, then surely we

Christians need to remember them as well. Uncritically, we often assume that because a person is rich, they must be enjoying the fruits of God's blessing. But this is not always the case. There are righteous and unrighteous rich and poor alike. And according to Luke and Acts, the way people treat their possessions provides a window into how much they love God.

Mary and Elizabeth are not shy about praising God, or for that matter, about blessing each other. Because of the widespread abuse of praise language, many Christians are reluctant about offering praise to God in the presence of others. Granted, taking care with what we say about God is a good thing, but be wary of the potential to become overly cautious—in other words, so concerned about misuse that we never overflow with praise to God at all. When was the last time we gushed about God's grace and good gifts? What are we waiting for?

What About Me?

• *The gospel produces joy.* The right—and *only*—response to what God has accomplished through Jesus is joy. What keeps you from experiencing joy this Advent season? Since God has blessed us with the coming of God's chosen one, what hinders our rejoicing? God was in Christ and all of us are blessed by his birth.

• *Your soul should magnify the Lord.* At some time in each of our lives, God has done marvelous things. And while none of these comes close to rivaling the Messiah's birth, God has repeatedly done the things mentioned in Mary's psalm. What has God done in your life that merits praise? Have you ever penned a psalm to God?

• *Elizabeth sees Mary as her friend, not her competitor.* Wise Elizabeth has no trouble blessing Mary as "the mother of my Lord" (1:43). Because she does not have a deep-seated need to be first, she is able to rejoice in her own circumstances, never once judging the gift of her son as second-rate. Too often we compare our own blessings to those enjoyed by others, and when we do this, somebody is bound to feel cheated. We need to take a lesson from Elizabeth, recognizing with due appreciation the great things we have been given by God.

• *God opposes the proud and remembers the lowly.* God will judge the proud, the powerful, and even the ungenerous rich. God also remembers the lowly, the hungry, and those who fear God. The Bible makes it quite clear that God is on the side of the underdog. Unfortunately, however, we Christians are not always on the side of God.

• *We need to have the courage to bless others.* Elizabeth blesses Mary, Jesus, and herself. Meanwhile, Mary exalts God and recalls God's greatness. Yet some of us have never blessed another person—unless, that is, it involved something more along the lines of "blessing out." Never lose sight of the fact that it takes much more courage to bless than it does to curse.

Resources

Raymond Brown, *The Birth of the Messiah* (Garden City NY: Doubleday, 1978).

Fred Craddock, *Luke* (Louisville: John Knox Press, 1990).

R. Alan Culpepper, "Luke," *New Interpreter's Bible*, vol. 9 (Nashville: Abingdon Press, 1995).

Earle E. Ellis, *The Gospel of Luke*, from The New Century Bible Commentary series (Grand Rapids: Eerdmans, 1974).

Craig A. Evans, *Luke*, from the New International Biblical Commentary series (Peabody MA: Hendrickson, 1990).

Joseph A. Fitzmyer, *The Gospel According to Luke* (I-IX), in Anchor Bible, vol. 28A (Garden City NY: Doubleday, 1983).

Luke Timothy Johnson, *The Gospel of Luke*, in Sacra Pagina, vol. 3 (Collegeville MN: Liturgical Press, 1991).

David L. Tiede, *Luke*, from Augsburg Commentary on the New Testament (Minneapolis: Augsburg, 1988).

LEAPING
FOR JOY
Luke 1:39-56

Introduction

Gabriel told Mary, "And now, your relative Elizabeth in her old age has also conceived a son; and this is the sixth month for her..." (Lk 1:36). Our text, however, does not explain how they were kin. Elizabeth was old—that is, far too old for the prospect of pregnancy to enter her mind. Mary, on the other hand, was young, too young to be expected to mother a child. Yet, by the Providence of God, these two women were bound together.

The text tells us that Mary lost no time making a beeline to Judea. "In those days Mary set out and went with haste to a Judean town in the hill country" (1:39). In fact, her visit was extended. "And Mary remained with her about three months and then returned to her home" (1:56). From this verse, we can infer that she stayed with Elizabeth until John was born. Traditionally labeled as "the Visitation," this episode...contains very little narrative. It consists almost entirely of inspired speech and song" (Fred Craddock, "Luke," *Interpretation*, Louisville: John Knox Press, 1990, 28).

Both the women in this account had an unusually clear sense of what God was about, including what God intended for the future. This especially impressed me, perhaps because so many of us just stumble through life, unsure as to the direction God is moving. We go to church, read our Bibles, and in general, go through all the motions of "being religious," but more often than not we act as mere "spectators" of the faith. Elizabeth and Mary, however, were more than exceptional; they were prophetic. We have a lot to learn from them.

Jesus Would Be Lord; John Would Prepare the Way, 1:43.

"And why has this happened to me, that the mother of my Lord comes to me?" (1:43). It seems Elizabeth knew long before John was born that his mission in life would be to prepare the way for Jesus. In other words, as most of us have always been taught, John was the forerunner, while Jesus was the main event. But when Jesus first went down to the Jordan to be baptized of John, this idea was far from obvious.

John the Baptizer was the first real prophet to burst onto the Jewish stage in centuries. He not only made news, but indeed, he *was* news! Defying customary procedures, he preached in remote places, dressed in strange clothes, kept an eccentric diet, and offended the mighty with his preaching. He didn't have to seek his audience, for the crowds sought him. So, just how powerful was his influence?

(1) "But Herod the ruler, who had been rebuked by him (John) because of Herodias, his brother's wife, and because of all the evil things that Herod had done, added to them all by shutting up John in prison" (Lk 3:19-20). Herod took his brother's wife, which John openly criticized as sin. For John's comments, Herod put him in prison—but the story doesn't stop there. Herodias wanted to kill John, but she was restrained by her husband, for "Herod feared John, knowing that he was a righteous and holy man, and he protected him. When he heard him, he was greatly perplexed; and yet he liked to listen to him" (Mk 6:20). Herodias eventually found a way to have John killed, but no doubt about it, John was known and heard by the most powerful people in the land.

(2) The Gospel writers tell us that the people inquired as to John's identity: "This is the testimony given by John when the Jews sent priests and Levites from Jerusalem to ask him, 'Who are you?' He confessed and did not deny it, but confessed, 'I am not the Messiah'" (Jn 1:19-20). When Jesus began to gather his own following, John was asked whether his own ministry would be threatened. His reply is classic: "He must increase, but I must decrease" (Jn 3:30). Whereas common people got Jesus and John confused, Elizabeth and Mary knew who was the greater of the

two from the very beginning. John was a great man, but Jesus was in a league of his own.

Mary Would Remember and Be Called "Blessed," 1:42, 48.

Elizabeth looked into the future with a vision that defied reason to see an obscure teenager, a "nobody from nowhere" rising in the estimate of humankind. "Blessed are you among women, and blessed is the fruit of your womb..." (1:42). Elizabeth got it right.

Occasionally, television movies tell of Roman emperors and other historical figures, such as Herod, Pilate, and the chief priests. If you take a moment to reflect, you will realize that all have nearly vanished into ancient history. In fact, when we do take the time to remember them, we notice that their stories are attached to Jesus, their fame ironically borrowed from the very same one they despised so passionately.

But Mary is another matter altogether. Churches by the thousands, colleges by the hundreds, grade schools around the world—all are named after Mary. "By the Middle Ages...hymns and prayers to Mary were widely used in both Eastern and Western Christianity, and belief in Mary's intercessory powers was widespread" (ed. Gordon S. Wakefield, *A Dictionary of Christian Spirituality*, London: SCM Press LTD, 1983, 258). Every day that goes by, millions of devout Catholics say their "Hail Marys," imploring Mary in their prayers for her gracious intercession. In fact, where Mary is concerned, Catholics hold the following doctrine:

• Mary was specially conceived (the Immaculate Conception; made official doctrine of the Church in 1854).
• At her death, she was taken up body and soul to heaven and reunited with her son (the Assumption; made official doctrine in 1950).

Whether or not you feel this goes beyond the scope of Scripture, you simply cannot keep from being amazed at the foresight of Elizabeth and Mary. They were just ordinary individuals. Granted, Elizabeth was the wife of a priest, but even that gave her little status. In the meantime, Mary was plucked from an obscurity that words cannot describe. And yet, these two women were so tightly wired to the ways of God until they could see into the future, correctly predicting fame for young Mary. It has come and flourished, just as they said it would.

What Elizabeth began as a hymn of praise to God and Mary in time has been deemed prophecy. And though the prophecies of Jeremiah and Ezekiel have come to pass, none rivals the predictions of Elizabeth and Mary. Their vision of the future came closer to what actually happened than that of any of the prophets who went before them. Elizabeth recognized Mary's faith and commends it to us today.

All the Old Testament Is Fulfilled in Jesus, 1:54-55.

"He has helped his servant Israel, in remembrance of his mercy, according to the promise he made to our ancestors, to Abraham and to his descendants forever" (1:54-55). Elizabeth and Mary tied the arrival of their sons to the fulfillment of all the promises God had made to Abraham, Isaac, and Jacob. And they were right. These women anticipated what would come to be one of the primary messages of the Early Church: the Old Testament was pointing to Jesus.

Elizabeth and Mary were not alone either. Simeon and Anna were in the Temple when the baby Jesus was "brought...up to Jerusalem to present him to the Lord" (Lk 2:22). The Holy Spirit had assured Simeon that he would not die until he "had seen the Lord's Messiah" (2:26b), so naturally when Mary and Joseph came into the Temple with the infant Jesus, Simeon took the baby in his arms and said, "Master, now you are dismissing your servant in peace, according to your word; for my eyes have seen your salvation,...a light for revelation to the Gentiles and for glory to your people Israel" (Lk 2:29-32).

Old Testament covenants were not just left hanging in the balance. Jesus built upon them and completed them. Jesus was not a denial of all that was Jewish; rather, he was the designed end of all God had been doing with Jews since God made covenant with Abraham (see Gen 12:1-3). So, even though Christians are New Testament people, we nevertheless have to acknowledge that the New Testament grows out of the Old.

Elizabeth and Mary had no Bible except the Old Testament, and they knew it backwards and forwards. Elizabeth and Mary, Simeon and Anna—all believed that God was at work in a special way among the Jewish people. And though the Jews had fallen upon hard times, God still had a special mission for them, and for that matter, would use them to redeem humankind. Elizabeth and Mary lived by hope, longing for Israel to be glorified. They saw their sons as agents in God's larger plan. John and Jesus would complete what Abraham and Moses began.

Most of us don't think on so grand a scale as Mary. We have small dreams, see no visions, and meanwhile, call ourselves realists. Our children feed on our practicality, rarely—if ever—rising to see themselves as "agents" in a plan that not only spans the ages, but also comes from the mind of God. This is a pity, especially when we consider that of all people, Mary should have been visionless. Besides, she was insignificant as far as the world was concerned, but she never saw herself that way. She set her sights high, and was important because she was about the work of God.

The Message of Jesus Would Elevate the Poor, 1:48-53.

"For he has looked with favor on the lowliness of his servant...He has scattered the proud in the thoughts of their hearts. He has brought down the powerful from their thrones, and lifted up the lowly; he has filled the hungry with good things, and sent the rich away empty" (1:48, 51-53). It is almost as if Mary were writing the sermon Jesus would preach when he came home to Nazareth: "The Spirit of the Lord is upon me, because he has anointed me to bring good news to the poor. He has sent me to proclaim release to the captives and recovery of sight to the blind, to let the oppressed go free, to proclaim the year of the Lord's favor" (Lk 4:18-19).

Fred Craddock said, "Luke expresses in sharpest focus what has been called a classical statement of God's activity: the lowly are raised and the lofty are brought low" (30). Clearly, God has a soft spot for the poor. According to all the Gospels, along with Paul (see 1 Cor 1:26-31) and James (see Jas 2:1-7), in the final judgment of God there will come "a reversal of fortunes; the powerful and rich will exchange places with the powerless and poor" (Ibid.). Mary anticipated this long before Jesus was born.

I suspect that what Mary said in the "Magnificat," she also taught Jesus as a boy. In fact, we can rest assured that some of Jesus' most profound teachings stemmed from his mother's instruction. And the point is this: God worked through Mary just as God works through our own parents to influence us. Is that all there is? Do we just marvel at Mary and Elizabeth and then go about our merry way? I hope not, for if we walk close enough to God, if we study the Scriptures reverently enough, if we listen for the whispers of the Holy Spirit, we too can see beyond ourselves to yield our lives to the larger designs of God. God is still at work. God is always looking for faithful people who are willing to bend to God's purposes.

Notes

Notes

4

IT'S YOUR TURN
TO CARRY THE BABY

Luke 2:1-20

Central Question

What will you do with the good news of Christ's birth?

Scripture

Luke 2:1-20 In those days a decree went out from Emperor Augustus that all the world should be registered. 2 This was the first registration and was taken while Quirinius was governor of Syria. 3 All went to their own towns to be registered. 4 Joseph also went from the town of Nazareth in Galilee to Judea, to the city of David called Bethlehem, because he was descended from the house and family of David. 5 He went to be registered with Mary, to whom he was engaged and who was expecting a child. 6 While they were there, the time came for her to deliver her child. 7 And she gave birth to her firstborn son and wrapped him in bands of cloth, and laid him in a manger, because there was no place for them in the inn. 8 In that region there were shepherds living in the fields, keeping watch over their flock by night. 9 Then an angel of the Lord stood before them, and the glory of the Lord shone around them, and they were terrified. 10 But the angel said to them, "Do not be afraid; for see—I am bringing you good news of great joy for all the people: 11 to you is born this day in the city of David a Savior, who is the Messiah, the Lord. 12 This will be a sign for you: you will find a child wrapped in bands of cloth and lying in a manger." 13 And suddenly there was with the angel a multitude of the heavenly host, praising God and saying, 14 "Glory to God in the highest heaven, and on earth peace among those whom he favors!" 15 When the angels had left them and gone into heaven, the shepherds said to one another, "Let us go now to Bethlehem and see this thing that has taken place, which the Lord has made known to us." 16 So they went with haste and found Mary and Joseph, and the child lying in the manger. 17 When they saw this, they made known what had been told them about this child; 18 and all who heard it were amazed at what the shepherds told them. 19 But Mary treasured all these words and pondered them in her heart. 20 The shepherds returned, glorifying and praising God for all they had heard and seen, as it had been told them.

Remembering

By now, it has been at least 15 months since Gabriel announced to Zechariah that Elizabeth was pregnant with a special child. Six months after that first announcement, the same messenger brought another word from God, except this time the message was for Mary, a young, unmarried woman. After learning that she would conceive the child of the Most High God, Mary rushed to Elizabeth's home in the hill country. Together they blessed each other and praised God. Mary stayed with her relatives for a full three months before leaving, at which point Elizabeth gave birth to a son. For the first time in the story, Zechariah honored God's wishes and named the child "John." Upon doing so, immediately and miraculously Zechariah regained his ability to speak. Only then could he sing a hymn of praise blessing the Most High, his newborn son, and the coming Messiah. As noted in previous sessions, Luke lends an artful symmetry to his story: two announcements—the first to Zechariah and the second to Mary— two hymns—Mary's first this time, then Zechariah's—and now, two births.

Studying

Luke's account of Jesus' birth supplies readers with quite a bit more detail than the other Gospel authors. And as we have seen before, Luke also provides all the names we could possibly need to know. The Roman emperor, the governor of Syria, David's city, the place where Joseph was living—Luke introduces us to all of them.

Since only imperfect records remain, historians have not yet been able to confirm exactly when and where the census occurred.

Of particular interest is the mention of Joseph in this lesson's passage, a rarity for Luke as well as his fellow Gospel writers. For example, in chapter 2 we see Joseph at Jesus' birth (v. 16), at the Temple when Jesus is presented (v. 33), and once again when Jesus is 12 years old (v. 48). Then in 4:22, when Jesus is rejected after his sermon at his home synagogue in Nazareth, the crowd wonders with nonchalant dismissal, "Isn't this Joseph's son?" Aside from these few references, however, we hear nothing more of Jesus' "stepfather."

Of all the Gospel writers, Matthew offers the most detail surrounding Joseph's contribution to Jesus' birth. Although he is not depicted in a speaking role, he acts kindly and decisively to protect Mary and her son.

Given the fact that Jesus' birth is one of the highlights of Luke's entire Gospel, we cannot help but notice the author's plain, unadorned account. At John's birth, Zechariah recovered his ability to speak, which was certainly nothing short of miraculous. Yet, the details of Jesus' birth are virtually uneventful, even "normal." In fact, while we have angels making a brilliant spectacle of announcing the Messiah's birth to poor shepherds, there is no mention whatsoever of any heavenly messengers at the place of his actual birth. For all the anticipation that has been built up over this special child, one might expect that Luke would have written a fuller, more elaborate version of the wondrous Nativity event.

So, why does Luke enlist such simple, unpretentious language for recounting this miraculous episode? A reader can never say with certainty what an author's intentions were during the composition of a piece, and surely Luke is no exception, but regardless, his oversimplified telling of our Savior's birth does seem to reinforce the message that God has come to the aid of the poor and the downtrodden. As Mary noted in her Magnificat, God has "lifted up the lowly [and] has filled the hungry with

good things" (1:52-53). Luke's Gospel reveals a deep concern for those who have been discarded or marginalized—people like the poor, the lame, the blind, the captive, and the oppressed. Even more accurately, Luke says that these are the very ones for whom God has a soft spot in the divine heart. These, who are the heirs of the promises made to Abraham and Sarah, were also the ones who most quickly recognized and acknowledged the Messiah's true identity. The simple, poor birth of God's only child reflects his relationship to those who have been banished to the outer margins of society, those whom God loves so deeply.

As further indication of the King of kings's very rustic and humble roots, Mary and Joseph place the newborn baby Jesus into a feedbox for animals. We have to wonder whether it was hard for a carpenter to submit his newborn son to such a rough-hewn piece of wood utility. Yet, here in a single image is the wonder of God's incarnation for the shepherds and all of Luke's audience to see: the Son of God in an animal feedbox, the Divine in an earthen vessel—a treasure in a trough.

The next seven short verses have been committed to memory, pondered, explored, and expanded upon countless times. Mary and Joseph swaddle the baby in "bands of cloth" (2:7), and although many assume that this was a common practice of the time, apparently the way Jesus was wrapped must have been unusual enough for the angel to have mentioned it to the shepherds (2:12). It is quite possible that what we have here is a hint of the Messiah's imminent death, especially when you consider that the dead were dressed for burial in much the same way—with bands of cloth.

The first to receive the good news of this holy birth are on-the-job shepherds, keeping watch in the cold of the night. An angel appears and says what we have come to expect angels to say: "Do not be afraid" (2:10). However, the shepherds are assured that this message is "good news of great joy for all the people" (2:10).

The angel goes on to give the baby three titles: Savior (or Healer), Messiah (the Greek meaning literally, "Christ"), and Lord (a term echoing both the emperor and the name of God in the Old Testament). Most North American Christians are more comfortable with the first two titles—Healer and Christ—than with the last. After all, if indeed Jesus is Lord, then he must be obeyed and followed, and who among us likes to live by someone else's terms?

Suddenly in the passage, there appears a heavenly army praising God. The New Revised Standard Version renders their joyous words: *Glory to God in the highest heaven, and on earth, peace among whom [God] favors* (2:14). This translation poses some difficulty, however, in that the final clause seems to limit God's peace to those "whom God favors." The Greek, on the other hand, lends itself to at least two other possibilities: "on earth, peace, the object of God's favor," or "on earth peace, with whom God is pleased." Either of these interpretations is better suited to the angel's declaration that this "good news of great joy" will be "for all people."

Upon delivery of the divine message, the shepherds run to Bethlehem to find the newborn child, and when they do, they relay for Jesus' parents what they have seen. Mary and Joseph are amazed, of course, for they have not seen any angels. But Mary treasures their words nevertheless, and will eventually come to grasp what they mean: that her son is the Messiah. Soon the shepherds return to their homeland, testifying to everyone who will listen about the remarkable birth they have witnessed. Never skeptical, they understand from the very start what to make of the baby, and so they carry his birth story with them wherever they go.

Understanding

Traditionally, the season of Advent carries three emphases: the first coming of Christ, his incarnation, and the anticipated return. This lesson's passage embraces all of these:

(1) Modern Christians must remember that first-century Jews deeply longed, yearned, and prayed for the Messiah's arrival. To

everyone's surprise, however, the sacred event panned out rather differently than people expected. After all, he was born into relative poverty. Instead of the powerful and the wise, shepherds and animals attended his birth. But even still, many religious people from that era met the news of Jesus' birth, life, death, and Resurrection with great joy. In fact, Acts says that literally tens of thousands came to follow him. What exactly does it mean that God's Messiah came into the world in this manner? Perhaps the same thing it means when Christ enters into our own lives in unexpected and unforeseen ways.

(2) We must remember our own lives *before* we can commit ourselves to Christ. Doing so might take us back seventy years or only a month. Regardless of how long ago it might have been, we need to remember our yearning for Christ to enter our lives. Recall your feelings when you first dedicated yourself to God. What was the condition of your life before the Messiah was born inside you? And by the same token, what was it afterwards? Was Christ's birth within you accompanied by "great joy"?

(3) The manner of Jesus' birth might very well indicate something about the manner in which he will return. We have at least two clues: not only did his birth transpire among the socially outcast, but in addition, a common element of surprise follows every mention of his return. Just as everyone was surprised the first time around, so will be the case when Christ returns. How do you live in light of Christ's second coming?

> As Jesus remarked in Matthew 25, the Son of God will know how much we love God by the extent to which we act out our love for our fellow humans—even the least of these.

What About Me?

- *The shepherds told everyone what they had seen and heard.* Their reaction to the news of the Messiah's birth involved far more than sentimental warmth. As a matter of fact, even now the shepherds continue to show us the way. They praised God and were eager to share the Messiah's incredible birth with others. Like them, will we also be willing to "carry the baby"?

- *The birth of Jesus is for all people.* The angel said, "I am bringing you good news of great joy for all the people" (2:10). Clearly, there is no room for question: all are included in this blessing.

- *Telling the story of Jesus' birth can be a natural extension of our joy.* The shepherds did not contemplate evangelism, nor did they consider how best to reach others with the good news. They simply told the story of Jesus as they experienced it—and to everyone they met! Granted, the story was fresh then, but now we know the whole of Jesus' life. Let us beware of our Christmas celebrations becoming too isolated. The story of Jesus continues only by our joyfully telling others.

- *Do not be afraid.* What are we afraid of? Do we need to be afraid of anything, since God is in Christ? If God is with us, who can be against us?

- *Joy is the most infallible sign of the presence of God.* Teilhard de Chardin, the great Christian mystic, said this 70 years ago, and his message still rings just as true today. We live in a time and culture that boasts lots of "pretty things" and impressive goings-on, but unfortunately, we are often left without much joy. Try not to lose sight of the fact that joy is God's gift to the world, a gift that we can either accept or reject. The choice is ours.

Resources

Raymond Brown, *The Birth of the Messiah* (Garden City NY: Doubleday, 1978).

Fred Craddock, *Luke* (Louisville: John Knox Press, 1990).

R. Alan Culpepper, "Luke," *New Interpreter's Bible*, vol. 9 (Nashville: Abingdon Press, 1995).

Earle E. Ellis, *The Gospel of Luke*, from The New Century Bible Commentary series (Grand Rapids: Eerdmans, 1974).

Craig A. Evans, *Luke*, from the New International Biblical Commentary series (Peabody MA: Hendrickson, 1990).

Joseph A. Fitzmyer, *The Gospel According to Luke* (I-IX), in Anchor Bible, vol. 28A (Garden City NY: Doubleday, 1983).

Luke Timothy Johnson, *The Gospel of Luke*, in Sacra Pagina, vol. 3 (Collegeville MN: Liturgical Press, 1991).

Karen Randolph Joines, "Passover," *Mercer Dictionary of the Bible*, ed. Watson E. Mills et al. (Macon GA: Mercer University Press, 1990).

David L. Tiede, *Luke*, from Augsburg Commentary on the New Testament (Minneapolis: Augsburg, 1988).

IT'S YOUR TURN
TO CARRY THE BABY

Luke 2:1-20

Introduction

Of all the stories in the Bible, perhaps none is so beautiful or memorable as the one we study now. Walter Russell Bowie wrote of our text, "There is haunting beauty in the manner of its telling; there is astonishing dramatic contrast; and from it flows a spiritual significance which all our wondering cannot exhaust" (*The Compassionate Christ: Reflections from the Gospel of Luke*, New York: Abingdon Press, 1965, 32). For 3 lessons we've been preparing for "Jesus' Birth." Now, we come to the main event.

Bottom line, familiarity makes us comfortable. For instance, we like hymns we've sung since childhood because they are familiar; we are *comfortable* with them. By the same token, I also enjoy old friends, especially the ones who know what's on my mind even when unspoken. But for all that is comfortable about familiarity, it can be a problem.

This lesson's text is read every Christmas. Some of us have probably heard it so often that we assume we've "got it," so to speak. Our minds can play tricks on us, which is why I'm so glad we've returned to Luke. Not only does he give more details, but he also tells the story with warmth and feeling. At any rate, the text still is seductive, in that Luke employs such well-turned phrases that it's easy to become *too* focused on the details. For instance, we've all heard sermons about there having been "no room in the inn." That circumstance is a detail. The main idea is Jesus. Doing my best to guard against becoming bogged down in the minor details, my goal is to present a full account of "Jesus' Birth" as offered by Luke.

Stage, 2:1-5.

"I decided, after investigating everything carefully from the very first, to write an orderly account for you, most excellent Theophilus, so that you may know the truth..." (Lk 1:3-4a). The Gospel of Luke is very meticulously written. Although staging is not what this story is about, before the main actor comes to centerstage, our author offers all sorts of background information:

(1) "A decree went out from Emperor Augustus that all the world should be registered" (2:1). Romans took a census every 14 years. In fact, we have "actual census documents written on papyrus and then discovered in the dust-heaps of Egyptian towns" (William Barclay, *The Gospel of Luke*, Philadelphia: Westminster Press, 1956, 15). The purpose of the census was both to compile an accurate tax list and to enroll men for military service. Jews, however, were not required to serve in the Roman army. Evidently, Luke believed the census was God's way of getting Joseph and Mary to Bethlehem. In that case, Augustus unwittingly set the stage for the birth of Jesus.

(2) "This was the first registration and was taken while Quirinius was governor of Syria" (2:2). Historians have not been able to confirm a census during the time Quirinius was governor, but most likely it was taken during this service as viceroy. William Barclay suggests that Jesus was born in 8 BC, which would make the church of the Middle Ages eight years off in their estimation.

(3) "All went to their own towns to be registered. Joseph also went from the town of Nazareth in Galilee to Judea, to the city of David called Bethlehem, because he was descended from the house and family of David" (2:3-4). This particular detail was very important to Luke. Luke's Jewish audience would be impressed to know that Jesus was ancestor to David, and interestingly enough, it was through Joseph's family lineage.

Joseph and Mary's journey from Nazareth to Bethlehem was a journey of 80 miles. Mary and Joseph were still engaged and she was expecting a child. It had to have been a very difficult trip for young Mary.

Birth, 2:6-7.

"While they were there, the time came for her to deliver her child. And she gave birth to her firstborn son and wrapped him in bands of cloth, and laid him in a manger, because there was no place for them in the inn" (2:6-7). Bethlehem was crowded, and there were plenty of others who had to "register" as well. Since Mary and Joseph had no friends or influence, they just had to take what they could find. To their dismay, the inn was full, but they were allowed to bunk with the animals in a place which may have been a cave or basement under a house.

And so it happened that the time came for the baby to be born. No angels attended, and neither did any miracles take place—at least, not blatant ones. God just stepped back and let things happen.

(1) The birth was normal, but the poverty of it all still touches us. The babe was pushed from the womb and put in a manger. Now, that's poverty at its worst. If anyone attended Mary except Joseph, there is no record of it. They were alone. Surely, we insist, someone would have witnessed their moment of need and given them their place in the inn, but that just didn't happen.

(2) Were there a newspaper in Rome, no one would have even noticed a headline about the birth of a Jewish boy in a remote province. But *we* do, for time has only magnified the importance of Christ. Obviously, contrast is a key device in Luke's account. Caesar was everything; Jesus was a nobody. Now, however, Jesus is a figure to be taken seriously, and just who is this Augustus character? Emperor Augustus is not lost entirely, but more books have been written about Jesus than about anyone else who ever lived. Compared to Jesus, Augustus was a man of modest fame at best. This is living proof that "many who are first will be last, and the last will be first" (Mt 19:30).

Interpretation, 2:8-14.

Luke assumed Joseph and Mary knew what was happening in the birth of Jesus. They had explanations in earlier announcements. But the rest of humankind needed some help, which again came by way of an angel: "In that region there were shepherds living in the fields, keeping watch over their flock by night. Then an angel of the Lord stood before them, and the glory of the Lord shone around them, and they were terrified" (2:8-9).

As William Barclay notes for us, "Shepherds were despised by the orthodox good people of the day. Shepherds were quite unable to keep the details of the ceremonial law...So the orthodox looked down on them as very common people" (17). Craddock said of the shepherds, "They belong on Luke's guest list for the kingdom of God: the poor, the maimed, the blind, the lame" ("Luke," *Interpretation*, Louisville: John Knox Press, 1990, 36).

The angel's appearance terrified the shepherds, much like Zechariah was frightened to death when Gabriel called (1:12) upon him. And then the interpretation began: "I am bringing you good news of great joy for all the people: to you is born this day in the city of David a Savior, who is the Messiah, the Lord...And suddenly there was with the angel a multitude of the heavenly host, praising God and saying, 'Glory to God in highest heaven, and on earth peace among those whom he favors'" (2:10b-14). Quickly the plot unfolded.

God was acting in a mighty way. This was good news indeed! The baby born in Bethlehem would be a Savior for *all* people. Now that the shepherds knew where the child was, all they had left to do was go and see him for themselves.

Confirmation, 2:15-18.

"When the angels had left them and gone into heaven, the shepherds said to one another, 'Let us go now to Bethlehem and see this thing that has taken place, which the Lord has made known to us.' So they went with haste and found Mary and Joseph, and the child lying in the manger...." What the angel said was completely true, for the shepherds saw the miracle of the baby Jesus with their own eyes. In fact, "seeing" becomes a frequent theme throughout the ministry of Jesus. The shepherds believed the angel, because the message relayed to them was confirmed by their own experience.

Good experience is the basis for Christian witness. Peter invited newborn Christians to grow up in the Lord, "if indeed you have tasted that the Lord is good" (1 Pet 2:3b). I know people who have quit church altogether just because of the mean-spirited ways of certain people who called themselves Christians. But I've never known anyone who could just walk away from Jesus. When we lead people to Jesus, they rarely turn away.

The whole Nativity episode energized the shepherds. "When they saw this, they made known what had been told them about this child; and all who heard it were amazed..." (2:17-18a). Besides, a shepherd's life is probably pretty routine. But I suspect this is one story they told over and over again until they were old men. Their grandchildren must have said, "Granddaddy, tell that story about the angel again." It was the one time they were more than mere keepers of sheep, as they were elevated to witness the mighty acts of God.

Reflection, 2:19-20.

"But Mary treasured all these words and pondered them in her heart" (2:19). What if Mary had written an account of what it was like to be the mother of Jesus? Now, *that* would be quite a story! But unfortunately, it's also one that was never put to paper. Instead, what we do have are hints that Mary kept a journal. Some of the material Luke records simply had to have come from Mary. For example, one of our clues comes after the trip to the Temple when Jesus was 12, the time Jesus lingered with the wise men. Finally, once all got back home to Nazareth, there follows, "His mother treasured all these things in her heart" (2:51b).

Every parent has a memory journal of the child-rearing years. Now that my wife and I are nearing old age, we look back on that time with nostalgia. It was a kind of magic time. To our daughter, Genie, we were all-wise, at least during this "era" in our lives. She leaned on us, trusted us, took our words as wisdom. I reflect on the times Genie and I walked around church buildings, locking doors, turning off air conditioners, closing windows. With her holding my hand, it was not a chore; it was an adventure. There was a time when my "coming home" was an event to Genie. That can brush away a lot of fatigue. These things I "treasure in my heart," just like any parent who has a stock of stories like mine.

Of course, Mary worked with a different kind of child. And while Jesus' birth is probably the holiest account of all time, there had to be parts of the whole story that brought great anxiety. Being the mother of Jesus was all at once wonderful and awful, as the baby in Bethlehem became the man who stood before Pilate, hung on a cross, suffered, and died. This lesson's text has been beautiful, but we know that Jesus' life was not without suffering.

Notes

Notes

5

A VISIT FROM
THE SUNRISE ON HIGH

Luke 1:57-80

Central Question

What role can you play in bringing God's salvation to all?

Scripture

Luke 1:57-80 Now the time came for Elizabeth to give birth, and she bore a son. 58 Her neighbors and relatives heard that the Lord had shown his great mercy to her, and they rejoiced with her. 59 On the eighth day they came to circumcise the child, and they were going to name him Zechariah after his father. 60 But his mother said, "No; he is to be called John." 61 They said to her, "None of your relatives has this name." 62 Then they began motioning to his father to find out what name he wanted to give him. 63 He asked for a writing tablet and wrote, "His name is John." And all of them were amazed. 64 Immediately his mouth was opened and his tongue freed, and he began to speak, praising God. 65 Fear came over all their neighbors, and all these things were talked about throughout the entire hill country of Judea. 66 All who heard them pondered them and said, "What then will this child become?" For, indeed, the hand of the Lord was with him. 67 Then his father Zechariah was filled with the Holy Spirit and spoke this prophecy: 68 "Blessed be the Lord God of Israel, for he has looked favorably on his people and redeemed them. 69 He has raised up a mighty savior for us in the house of his servant David, 70 as he spoke through the mouth of his holy prophets from of old, 71 that we would be saved from our enemies and from the hand of all who hate us. 72 Thus he has shown the mercy promised to our ancestors, and has remembered his holy covenant, 73 the oath that he swore to our ancestor Abraham, to grant us 74 that we, being rescued from the hands of our enemies, might serve him without fear, 75 in holiness and righteousness before him all our days. 76 And you, child, will be called the prophet of the Most High; for you will go before the Lord to prepare his ways, 77 to give knowledge of salvation to his people by the forgiveness of their sins. 78 By the tender mercy of our God, the dawn from on high will break upon us, 79 to give light to those who sit in darkness and in the shadow of death, to guide our feet into the way of peace." 80 The child grew and became strong in spirit, and he was in the wilderness until the day he appeared publicly to Israel.

Remembering

Throughout the progression of Advent, we have examined Luke's approach to telling the story of Jesus' birth. As you may remember, he introduces his Gospel with a dedication to Theophilus, which certainly could have been the name of a real person, but just as easily may have been Luke's generic term for anyone who loves God. You will also recall that Luke opens with the story of Zechariah and Elizabeth, who desperately want a child, although Zechariah is skeptical when the angel Gabriel tells him that the couple's wish will indeed be fulfilled. So, in order to give Zechariah the proof he demands, Gabriel lends credence to his celestial authority by striking the old priest mute, just reward for his mistrust in God's divine message.

Six months after his appearance to Zechariah, the angel appears once again to announce a miraculous conception, only this time he approaches a young, unmarried Jewish girl named Mary. Of course, Mary is surprised and curious to know more, but unlike Zechariah, she willingly and eagerly accepts God's plan. In fact, after the angel departs, she rushes to her relative Elizabeth's house, where the two pregnant women rejoice together over the impending births of their first children. In fact, it is during this visit that Mary voices what has come to be deemed a sacred hymn of praise.

The account of John's birth and naming, including Zechariah's song, is only the first half of a pair of birth stories. The second one, which relays the birth of the Messiah, we studied last chapter. Coincidentally, this chapter's story is also the second phase of a coupling of praise songs. As we have already discussed prior, Mary gave the first one. But before we leave our study of Jesus' birth altogether, we first need to take a closer look at Zechariah's hymn of praise.

Studying

We should not be too quick to judge Zechariah. It is quite possible that he just didn't understand his role in the "big picture," the cosmic drama of salvation. Little did he know that he would soon become the father of the last prophet ever to precede *the* Messiah. In fact, according to Gabriel, this child would be blessed with both the power and the spirit of Elijah, turning the hearts of parents to their children, turning the disobedient to the wisdom of the righteous, and above all else, making the people prepared for the Lord (1:17). Granted, this would not ensure the son's popularity with people in power, but then again, very few true prophets ever "get in good" with the authorities anyway.

As most people do upon learning that a mother and child have made it through labor successfully, Elizabeth's neighbors rejoiced at the great mercy God had shown her (1:58). Eight days later, the boy was circumcised, a ritual called a *bris* by contemporary Jews, and following in the tradition of the covenant made to Abraham. As part of the *bris* ceremony, often performed at home, the baby is placed on the chair that has been reserved for Elijah in the Seder meal. As the newborn is placed into position, the rabbi says, "Who knows, but maybe this child is Elijah, the prophet who will herald the coming of the messiah?"

> Today the Seder features a ritual designed to retell the biblical story of the Exodus. Part of the tradition involves setting the Seder table with place settings for all the guests, including an extra one for Elijah, the absent guest.

After the birth of his child, Zechariah is treated by the community in much the same way that he treated Gabriel upon the announcement of John's birth: the ones who *should* believe him are actually the ones who *don't*! Naturally, everyone encourages the couple to name the child after his father, but Elizabeth refuses, giving him the name assigned by God (1:13). Yet, clearly her word is not enough to satisfy onlookers, because they use gestures to signal to Zechariah that his opinion is warranted. At this point, Zechariah communicates the decisive command by writing, "His name is John" (1:63). All are amazed, Luke says, but not as amazed as they will be at Zechariah's next display. Immediately after affirming his son's name as "John," the old priest regains his voice and begins to praise God, wishing that he had reacted in similar fashion from the outset.

The fact that Zechariah's friends use gestures may indicate that Zechariah was deaf as well as mute.

As to be expected, the neighbors become very afraid, allowing their imaginations to run wild as they try to predict what sort of person this child will become. None of their illusions, however, are even halfway wild enough. Not a single one among them has vision enough to foresee that this newborn will go on to become a honey-and-locust-eating wilderness prophet, the likes of whom have not been seen in Israel since Elijah.

Then all of a sudden Zechariah is filled with the Holy Spirit, just as his wife had been three months earlier. Like Mary before him, Zechariah issues a psalm full of praise and wonder, often called the "Benedictus" (meaning "blessed") after the first word in the Latin translation. And as was the case with Mary's Magnificat, there also are several noteworthy themes in Zechariah's spectacular psalm.

First, the new father echoes Mary's reminder that God has been faithful about keeping promises. Just as "the holy prophets of old" foretold, in the line of David, God has raised up "a horn of salvation" (1:69-70). And above all else, God remembers the holy covenant "promised to our ancestors" (1:72), and honors the oath sworn "to our ancestor Abraham" (1:73). As a matter of fact, this is a frequently occurring contrast theme in Luke's writings: God remembers and consequently honors all promises made. How appropriate, then, that Zechariah's name means, "Yahweh has remembered"!

A second overriding theme in Zechariah's psalm is God's mercy. After all, the scope of this story is possible in the first place only because of God's initiation and mercy. In other words, we are neither responsible for nor deserving of God's grace and gifts; rather, the Creator freely gives them to us. Although Elizabeth's friends and neighbors wonder at God's "great mercy to her" (1:58), this actually is the very same mercy that was shown to their ancestors (1:72)—not to mention, the same mercy that would be inherited through the coming of the Messiah: *By the tender mercies of our God, the dawn from on high will break upon us* (1:78). We noted before that one of Luke's main themes is the link between the Old Testament story of God's love and what God is doing now through Elizabeth and Zechariah, as well as what God will do in Jesus. It is this distinct connection of past, present, and future that has motivated Christians through-out time to tell and re-tell the gospel story.

A third theme in the Benedictus is John's role in calling the people to prepare for the coming of the Most High, which he plans to do by leading them to repentance, proclaiming in Luke 3:3 a baptism of repentance for the forgiveness of sins. It is John's mission to soften the people's hearts, in order that Jesus may capture them.

The fourth motif that we discover in Zechariah's song—as well as one we have already touched upon—is the echo of Old Testament language. Consult almost any Bible translation and you will discover many citations, allusions, and echoes just in these 12 verses alone (1:68-79). Luke's reason for employing Old Testament turns-of-phrase is to emphasize that the same God who acted in history is doing so again. Also, be sure to take note of the two verses of particularly stunning elegance in the psalm,

> A highly developed theme in Luke's writings is the necessity for repentance in the face of God's grace.

as Zechariah predicts that the Messiah will be the dawn of God's great love breaking on the people:

> By the tender mercy of our God,
> The dawn from on high will break upon us,
> To give light to those who sit in darkness and in the shadow of
>   death,
> To guide our feet into the way of peace. (1:78-79)

Could there be a more worthy or suitable benediction to Jesus' birth than this? While we are often well acquainted with a number of the beautiful passages in our Bible, these two verses have been overlooked by many. The image is of a group of people groping in the dark to find the path, when suddenly the dawn breaks from behind high mountains to illuminate the way. Like other parts of Zechariah's hymn, these words echo Psalm 23: *Even if I pass through the valley of the shadow of death, you are with me.* Few people have been lucky enough to avoid getting lost in such a valley or stranded along one of life's winding roads, but by God's tender mercy, we often manage to make our way back to peace.

Understanding

Eventually, Zechariah comes to understand his part in God's plan of salvation for all people. Filled with the Holy Spirit, the old priest sees the sweep of God's mercy, and in fact, is truly honored that he will be the father of the new Elijah, the herald of the son of the Most High. As this year closes, ask yourself: What is *my* part in bringing God's marvelous mercy to others? Do I, like Zechariah, have trouble believing that God is at work in and through me? Do I ever take a moment to remember what God has done in my life and in the life of my church throughout the last year?

Many of us may not be happy with the roles we think God has called us to play. However, many of our roles are self-chosen. What endeavors dare you undertake in the name of God's tender mercy during the coming year? What tiresome role might you cast aside for the sake of "freshening up" God's call? Luke's Gospel is intended to set people free in the name of Jesus. Whom do you know that has lost their way in darkness, and likewise, how can you reflect God's light for them?

Looking back, we can often discern those times when God has lifted us out of the darkness. God is continually lighting our way and guiding our feet toward the path of peace. Both psalms discussed highlight what God *has* done, what God *is currently doing*, and what God *will* do for God's people. Perhaps if we were to take the time to open ourselves to the Holy Spirit, we too might experience the "sweep of grace," thereby gaining a bit more insight into what we can contribute to God's plan of salvation.

What About Me?

• *We don't always understand God's intentions initially.* Such was the case with Zechariah, who had nine months of silence to re-evaluate his response to Gabriel's message. The last words out of his mouth voiced his suspicion, but now, his first words are of faith. Many of us need several tries to figure out what God is doing in the world, except for most of us it takes longer than nine months to learn from our mistakes.

• *Zechariah gradually came to understand his part in the cosmic drama.* God wanted neither Zechariah nor John to be the Messiah. In fact, God's plan had already been set long before they so much as considered entering the world. However, each of us has a significant part to play in advancing the Kingdom, and God needs us to play it well—with faith and courage alike.

• *Today is a fine day to reconsider the direction and meaning of your life.* Zechariah assumed that the best years of his life were over. In truth, though, the most important part of his life was only beginning: raising his son, John, to act as God's herald to the chosen one, the son of God. What does God want to do in *your* life this year? What is God trying to accomplish that you are resisting?

• *Memorize the final words of Zechariah's psalm.* These will be of comfort to anyone who remembers them. Let each word bubble within your soul like a fresh mountain spring:
  By the tender mercy of our God,
  The dawn from on high will break upon us,
  To give light to those who sit in darkness and in the shadow of
    death,
  To guide our feet into the way of peace. (1:78-79)

Resource

Raymond Brown, *The Birth of the Messiah* (Garden City NY: Doubleday, 1978).

Fred Craddock, *Luke* (Louisville: John Knox Press, 1990).

R. Alan Culpepper, "Luke," *New Interpreter's Bible*, vol. 9 (Nashville: Abingdon Press, 1995).

Earle E. Ellis, *The Gospel of Luke*, from The New Century Bible Commentary series (Grand Rapids: Eerdmans, 1974).

Craig A. Evans, *Luke*, from the New International Biblical Commentary series (Peabody MA: Hendrickson, 1990).

Joseph A. Fitzmyer, *The Gospel According to Luke* (I-IX), in Anchor Bible, vol. 28A (Garden City NY: Doubleday, 1983).

Luke Timothy Johnson, *The Gospel of Luke*, in Sacra Pagina, vol. 3 (Collegeville MN: Liturgical Press, 1991).

Karen Randolph Joines, "Passover," *Mercer Dictionary of the Bible*, ed. Watson E. Mills et al. (Macon GA: Mercer University Press, 1990).

David L. Tiede, *Luke*, from Augsburg Commentary on the New Testament (Minneapolis: Augsburg, 1988).

A VISIT FROM
THE SUNRISE ON HIGH

Luke 1:57-80

Introduction

With this session, we may end not only a unit but an entire year
as well. It has been a good study. Usually Christmas lessons drive
us to Bethlehem, where we take a close look at the shepherds,
wise men, and angels—and we did some of that. But in a way I
can't explain, this unit has made me think thoughts I've never
thought before. I've looked at the people God chose to be players
in this great drama. Who were these people that they should be
so honored?

This lesson's text isn't often preached or taught. We pass over
it for the "important parts" of the Christmas story. But sometimes the Bible digresses to offer us *real* insight. The meat of our
text is not the birth of John or even his naming, but rather, the
prophecy of Zechariah. When he confirmed that his son was to be
named John, the Spirit loosed his tongue and allowed him to
proclaim some very profound ideas.

Most modern Americans are lost. They don't know where they
came from or where they are going. And even for those who
aren't entirely lost—spiritually or otherwise—the "lostness" of
our neighbors can influence us just as negatively as it would if it
were our own. Sometimes, we cannot help but wonder about the
"old" ideas we learned at church when we were children. Are they
really true? Does anybody even believe that stuff anymore?

Then along comes Zechariah, preaching joyous declarations
that we all need to hear and pass on. He is not diminished by
either self-doubt or God-doubt. On the contrary, his spirit is
loosed and enlarged by his faith. He is the man I want to be. He's
the individual our people long to be when they get up on Sunday

morning and dress for church. They don't need much help in sorting out a lot of the stuff they hear in worship services; it is the big picture that is missing.

Heritage Defines Us, 1:68-73.

"Blessed be the Lord God of Israel, for he has looked favorably on his people and redeemed them" (1:68). Heritage defined Zechariah, for he genuinely believed that he was one of God's people. In fact, he perceived his own history as holy history. Israel was not just another of the several tribes that dotted the Middle East. Israel was set apart. They were a people who were in covenant with God. As Zechariah put it, "He has shown the mercy promised to our ancestors, and has remembered his holy covenant" (1:72).

Zechariah came of people who were, to be very blunt, dirt poor. They were on the bottom rung of nations, and were of no account by any worldly measure. Even though Zechariah may have thought of himself as having a great heritage, he had next to nothing in the present. And like it or not, you can't eat heritage. Why didn't the man come into the real world? And yet, all the while it was his heritage that sustained him. In fact, it was heritage that sustained all the characters of Jesus' birth story. Modern Americans, on the other hand, lean too much on skills and education and not enough on who we are and where we came from.

However, Jews—those living then as well as those living now—put great stock in ancestry. The psalmist wrote, "The Lord is my chosen portion and my cup; you hold my lot. The boundary lines have fallen for me in pleasant places; I have a goodly heritage" (Ps 16:5-6).

Notice how many times in the Old Testament people are called to recollect certain events. Remember how God brought Israel out of Egypt? Passover has become the memorial for this event. We are children of Judaism. When Jesus came to Passover, he redefined "deliverance." No longer did it refer to a people struggling to escape Egypt, but instead, came to embrace deliverance for all people from the sin that enslaves us. In fact, this is why we celebrate the Lord's Supper. On the Lord's Supper table at our church is the phrase, "This do in remembrance of me." And by our doing so, we enjoy our own heritage celebration—remembering something from the past that defines us.

If you move, let family ties slide, or live for the present long enough, pretty soon you will realize that any heritage you had to begin with has been lost. There is nothing but sheer poverty in this kind of life. Keep in mind, Zechariah had nothing. He was but a Jew who had slight standing in the larger social order. But he knew who he was. He knew where he came from. Therefore, he also was connected to God in a profound way because he had a past (a heritage), he had a future.

Many of us can "connect" with Zechariah, because we come of rural, poor, uneducated people. Most of us have had opportunities our grandparents never had, and by their standards, we've "got it made." But in another sense, we may be poorer than they. They lived their faith mightily. In many ways, they were like Zechariah; their religious heritage defined them.

God's Character Becomes Our Own, 1:70-74, 78.

A basic rule of religion says that the devotees of a particular faith eventually become like the god(s) they worship. More specifically, if we worship a good and loving God—as we do—that can be a very good thing. Zechariah told us about the nature of God in his prophecy:

(1) God keeps promises. For instance, the covenant that God made with Abraham was renewed with Isaac and Jacob. God was promised to Israel, and in turn, Israel was promised to God. History tells the sad story of Israel's more than occasional falling away from God and worshipping idols instead. In fact, this is a major theme among the prophets of the Old Testament. But God is not like Israel. Sometimes God punishes, but by the same token, is always willing to forgive and start over again—that is, if repentance is authentic. If our God keeps promises, shouldn't we do the same?

(2) God shows mercy. For all the hard times that had plagued Israel, from a history that was sometimes brutal, Zechariah discerned a God who was kind and gentle. When they were down,

there came a prophet to lift their spirits and refresh the vision of God. Likewise, whenever they were in dire straits, they were delivered. This was their history, clearly a story of one merciful gesture after another.

Jesus taught us a rule to live by: If God has been good to us, then we are to be good to someone else. If God has forgiven us, then we are to forgive each other. If God has been merciful to us, then we are to be merciful to others. Of course, Christians are divided over what some would call excessive mercy. But regardless, it's the nature of God, and sooner or later it needs to come out in the nature of me.

(3) Zechariah did not come right out and say that God was holy; however, he did say "that we, being rescued from the hands of our enemies, might serve him without fear, in holiness and righteousness before him all our days" (1:74-75). So, where did Zechariah get his notions of what "holiness and righteousness" entail? Quite simply, he borrowed them from the nature of God.

The peculiar, special, unique feature of Israel's God was ethical holiness. Other nations hailed gods that asked them to sacrifice, while still other gods were thought to be in control of harvest and battle. But those gods rarely had any sense of the ethical. Israel's God demanded worship and loyalty, surely, but Israel's God also asked for much more. To worship Yahweh was to worship a God who was honest, faithful, merciful, and just. To worship One of such stature, we must follow in God's footsteps.

Many of us want the benefits of religion without the rigor. In other words, we crave "cheap grace." We truly *want* to go to heaven; we just aren't too keen on being ethical all the time. Besides, it's so much more appealing to reduce entrance to heaven to "believing in Jesus." But Matthew 25:31-46 is still in the Bible. Jesus himself said it, and despite the fact that some preachers try to make it go away, it's still there. Because God is holy, so should we be, too.

Zechariah had a picture of God in his mind that shaped his perception of the world in general. That picture of God did not just hang on Zechariah's living room wall; it was the very model for his life. That's why Luke tells us about him in the first place.

God's Future Becomes Our Mission, 1:76-80.

The old priest Zechariah seems to ascend in our text. Only a matter of months ago, he had trouble taking in the promise of Gabriel that a son would come to him and his wife. It was a momentary faith failure, granted, but he recovered nonetheless. Listen as he tells about God's future:

(1) "And you, child, will be called the prophet of the Most High; for you will go before the Lord to prepare his ways, to give knowledge of salvation to his people by the forgiveness of their sins" (1:76-77). Zechariah and Elizabeth had borne a son, but like Elkanah and Hannah, they were giving him back to the Lord (see 1 Sam 1:21-28). Obviously, Zechariah could see the future better than most of us can see the present. He realized early in the game that his son was a major piece in the intricate puzzle God was putting together. The child was destined to "go before the Lord to prepare his ways," and so he did, at which point God's future became John's mission.

(2) "By the tender mercy of our God, the dawn from on high will break upon us, to give light to those who sit in darkness and in the shadow of death, to guide our feet into the way of peace" (1:78-79). I do not argue that Zechariah foresaw either the Early Church or Pentecost. That's asking too much. But I will assert that he had at least some idea that there would come a new salvation to humankind through John and Jesus. God was working through "little" lives to accomplish big goals.

This is the missing piece in much of modern Christianity. Although we do a good job of maintaining the Church, we tend to lose sight of our actual *mission*. And certainly the majority of us can't even imagine that our kids could be God's agents to bring in a new order, much less the Kingdom of God. "The dawn from on high will break upon us" is strong stuff. Zechariah didn't believe in the end of the world; he insisted that God was about the redemption and reformation of our world. And best of all, God needed Zechariah's boy to get the job done. Zechariah didn't argue with God, mind you, for he had a vision, and "without a vision, the people perish" (Prov 28:18 KJV).

Zechariah and Elizabeth, Joseph and Mary—these were some poor people. Simply put, they were nobodies. But in truth, they actually stood on higher ground than most of us, in that they truly believed in their heritage. In fact, it defined them. They also wanted more than anything else to emulate the nature of their God. They truly believed God was doing a new thing; they were sincerely honored to be a part of the mission. So long as we have a few able "Zechariahs" in our churches, we should be just fine.

Notes

Notes

www.ingramcontent.com/pod-product-compliance
Lightning Source LLC
Chambersburg PA
CBHW070552030426
42337CB00016B/2456